BLESSED AMONG WOMEN

EXPLORING THE VIRGIN MARY'S TRUE ROLE IN GOD'S PLAN FOR SALVATION

PAUL LINDQUIST

Copyright © 2006 by Paul Lindquist

Blessed Among Women
by Paul Lindquist

Printed in the United States of America

ISBN 1-60034-627-8

All rights reserved solely by the author. The author guarantees all contents are original and do not infringe upon the legal rights of any other person or work. No part of this book may be reproduced in any form without the permission of the author. The views expressed in this book are not necessarily those of the publisher.

Unless otherwise indicated, Bible quotations are taken from the New International Version of the Holy Bible. Copyright © 1973, 1978, 1984 by International Bible Society.

www.xulonpress.com

CONTENTS

	Introduction	ix
1	The Supremacy of Scripture	11
2	The Church's Official Positions on Sacred Scripture and Mary	25
3	Mary: The Perfect Realization of the Faith	33
4	The Immaculate Conception	37
5	Mary's Perpetual Virginity and Assumption	45
6	Mary: "Mediatrix of all Graces"	53
7	Queen of Heaven and Coredemptrix	61
8	The Apparitions of Mary	71
9	In Pursuit of the Truth	79
10	Why the Truth Matters to Our Salvation	83

Dedication

To my wife, Angelina, and my mother, Dorothy. Without you both I would never be anything close to the person I am today. Thank you for all you've done for me.

Introduction

As a lifelong Catholic, I was raised with an underlying respect and reverence for Mary. However, I was also taught by my mother not to pray to anyone else but God. While my mom taught me not to pray to Mary, the nuns at Catholic school taught just the opposite.

This inevitably led to a conflict in my personal theology. For years, I shrugged off the differences as no big deal. However, in recent years, the Lord has placed the task on my heart of resolving these beliefs and hopefully helping others that have similar questions.

Let me start by saying I love the Catholic Church. I am blessed by God to have been placed in this denomination, and I would not trade it for anything. I believe most of what the Church teaches, and I especially subscribe to the Nicene Creed, the core doctrine of the Church.

The Catholic Church is truly a God-ordained institution, and I have been able to find the everlasting peace of knowing Jesus Christ as my Lord and Savior within the Church.

Some may ask, why bother with this little question about Mary's role in the Church and ultimately in God's plan for salvation? After all, whether a person is saved or not doesn't depend on whether or not someone prays to Mary, does it?

Well, that's where the conflict arises. It appears there are many Catholics who believe that salvation *is* dependant on devotion to Mary. Many call her *Mediatrix of all Graces, Coredemptrix,* and *Queen of Heaven.* Although not all of these terms for Mary are official Catholic dogma (yet), Mary is thought of this way by millions of Catholics worldwide.

So what is Mary's true role in God's plan for the salvation of humanity? That is the key critical question in my mind and the focus of this book. Most Christians can agree that she is the most blessed among women (although you wouldn't know that in many Protestant denominations).

What I hope we learn by the end of this book is whether or not Mary's position goes beyond just being the greatest of role models and God's vehicle for bringing the savior into the world.

My prayer for everyone who reads this book is that it would bring them closer to God's truth and help them develop a stronger relationship with Jesus Christ. Please read this book with an open mind and pray that the Holy Spirit gives you wisdom and discernment in what you are reading.

By the way, some of you may be wondering, *Who is this guy, and what are his qualifications to write such a book?* I have to confess that I'm nobody special. I'm not a priest or a deacon, and I'm not currently studying to be either one. I'm just a lay person who happens to be in relentless pursuit of the truth, wherever that leads.

My only qualification is that I've humbly given this work to the Lord. I've asked Him to be my guide throughout this writing. My only purpose in writing this book is to help bring others (and myself) closer to God's truth. As Jesus said, "you shall know the truth, and the truth shall set you free" (John 8:32).

Thank you in advance for reading what I have to say.

CHAPTER 1

The Supremacy of Scripture

When exploring Mary's role in God's plan for salvation, we need to start by finding out what God has to say about it. In order to find God's thoughts on the subject, the first place to look would be God's Word as written in the Bible. This raises questions for some, and these questions need to be answered before we can explore this topic further.

The first of these questions is where did the Bible come from? The second is can the Bible be trusted? And the third question is does the Bible have total doctrinal authority or can the Catholic Church make a proclamation that is contrary to it? We will try to answer all of these questions in this first chapter.

1. Where did the Bible come from?

The Bible is a collection of writings from roughly forty different authors over a period of fifteen hundred to two thousand years. It was written on three continents and in three different languages.

Most of the authors of these writings were Jewish, and we believe that all of the writings that made it into the canon of Scripture were inspired by God. This canon of Scripture was assembled by the early Church within the first few hundred years of Christ's death and resurrection.

So the Bible came out of the many councils of the early Church. These early Church fathers fought vehemently to protect what they believed to be the Word of God. Many writings were rejected along the way. Some of these writings were heretical, and others were determined to just not meet the high criteria required to be considered the inspired Word of God.

Amazingly, the Bible has been preserved in its present form for nearly two thousand years. Despite the attempts of Roman emperors to stamp out Christianity, and despite other persecutions throughout the centuries, the Bible and Christianity have endured.

Today, this book has been read by millions of people, and there are more copies in print than any other book in the world. It is estimated that there are between two and three billion Christians worldwide and they all hold this book to be their standard. This is likely a testament to the fact that the Bible is indeed a divinely inspired book.

As mentioned earlier, the Bible had forty different authors from all walks of life. Some were shepherds, others were kings, and still others were prophets and disciples. With all these different perspectives from different time periods, the fact that the message remained consistent suggests that this book is more than just the work of the human authors that wrote it. This book is inspired by God.

The section of the Bible known as the New Testament is a collection of writings covering the life of Jesus and the early Church. It contains twenty-seven books and letters written over roughly a fifty-year period. It is divided into two main sections: The Gospels and Acts & the Letters.

The four Gospels were written by four different authors. These authors gave their perspectives on the life and teachings of Jesus Christ. The book called Acts of the Apostles was written by Luke, author of one of the four Gospels. This book provides a history of the early Church, starting with the event known as Pentecost, when the Holy Spirit descended upon the twelve apostles.

The Letters were written around the same time as the Gospels and Acts. The majority of the Letters were written by the apostle Paul. Others were written by Peter, James, John, and Jude, all of whom were either apostles or relatives of Jesus.

When the canon of Scripture was being assembled by the early Church, they used three main criteria for a work's acceptance as part of the New Testament. These criteria were: consistency with orthodox theology, widespread acceptance throughout all the churches of that time period, and that they were written by an apostle of Jesus Christ or someone with a direct connection to an apostle of Jesus Christ.

The first criterion for an acceptable work of Scripture in the New Testament was the need to be consistent with orthodox Christian theology. The early Church had a lot of different writings to consider, and many were able to be eliminated using this first criterion. These were false writings that were simply heretical and contradicted what was accepted as true orthodox Christian theology.

Many documents that sounded authentic were rejected based on this criterion. For example, the early Church rejected the Acts of John and the Gospel of Thomas because they simply weren't consistent with their teachings. Their names sought to give them credibility, but they were likely not written by either John or Thomas. The teachings in these writings were part of the Gnostic heresy that was popular a couple hundred years after Christ's resurrection.

The second criterion for a writing being part of the canon of Scripture was having widespread acceptance throughout all the churches of that time period. Some very difficult decisions had to be made using this standard.

There were many writings that were fairly consistent with Church theology but were not given merit by all the churches. This meant that these were good writings, just not divinely inspired writings. Some examples of these writings included the Shepherd of Hermas and the Letter of Barnabas.

The third criterion for acceptance in the canon of Scripture for the New Testament was that the writing had to be directly from an apostle or someone associated with an apostle. This also meant the document would have been from the earliest time period in the Church's existence.

As we know from what ended up being accepted as part of the New Testament, every one of these books has a direct connection to Jesus Christ because they were all written by apostles or associates of apostles, and they can all be dated to within roughly a generation of Jesus' death and resurrection.

In case the other two criteria weren't stringent enough, this last one made it even more exclusive. There were a lot of fine writings by many of the early church fathers that couldn't be included in the Bible simply because these writers had not walked the earth with Jesus or been mentored by someone who had walked the earth with Jesus.

In the case of the Old Testament, all of these are Jewish writings, many of which have been in existence for thirty-five hundred to four thousand years. The Old Testament contains thirty-nine books and is divided into four sections: The Torah, Israel's history, Poetry and Wisdom, and the Prophets.

The first five books known as the Torah are the most sacred Jewish writings and are thought to be the writings of Moses. They begin in Genesis with the creation story and end with the Israelites in the desert preparing to cross the Jordan River and conquer the Promised Land.

The second section of the Old Testament known as Israel's history has twelve books by several different authors. These writings cover much of Israel's history before Christ.

They begin in the book of Joshua as the Israelites enter the Promised Land. They go on to cover, from a historical perspective, Israel's progression from being governed by judges to kings to being conquered by other surrounding nations.

The third section of the Old Testament is called Poetry and Wisdom. This section contains five books, three of which were written by Solomon, David's son and the king of Israel during her most prosperous period of time. These books contain eternal wisdom about topics ranging from human suffering to falling in love, giving God's perspective on these issues.

The final (and longest) section of the Old Testament is known as the Prophets. This is a collection of seventeen books written by God's prophets during various time periods in Israel's history before Christ.

Many of these prophets brought word of God's impending judgment for violating His laws, while others brought words of encouragement when times were tough and the Israelites were in captivity.

There is an additional section of the Old Testament that has been in dispute throughout the centuries. It is known as the Apocrypha. This section is *not* considered Scripture by the Jews or Protestant Christians, but has been accepted by the Catholic and Eastern Orthodox Churches.

The Apocrypha is a collection of eleven books written between 300 B.C. and 70 A.D., which include a variety of types of writings from history to wisdom literature. Though these writings were familiar to early Christians, they were not included in St Jerome's 4th century A.D. translation of the Bible into Latin.

The Catholic Church later translated The Apocrypha into Latin and accepted them as part of Scripture. This acceptance was reaffirmed at the Council of Trent in 1546 A.D. in response to the Protestant Reformation and the Protestants' rejection of these books.

Despite the difference in perspectives of the authors and the fifteen hundred plus years of difference in the time periods of these authors, the messages of the Bible are largely the same. Every book in the Bible has one thing in common: it testifies to God's plan of salvation for humanity.

2. Can the Bible be trusted?

The Bible was not only written and put together in a way that implies divine inspiration, it has also proven itself by being accurate in all of its historical writings and prophecies. To date, we know of no historical event or prophetic writing in the Bible that has been contradicted by outside evidence.

By contrast, all the history that is written about in the Bible is accurate and most of the prophecies have been fulfilled or are in the process of being fulfilled.

There has been a mountain of research and many books published in recent years on the historical and archeological reliability of the Bible. An outstanding book written by Lee Strobel called *The Case for Christ* deals with much of the outside evidence for the existence of Jesus Christ and His death and resurrection as described in the four Gospels of the New Testament.

Strobel, the author, is a former devout atheist turned Christian, and he lays out in detail the facts that support the reasonable conclusion that Jesus Christ really is who He says He is: God in human form.

This book also gives evidence that Jesus Christ actually did the things the Gospels say He did, including dying on the cross for the sins of humanity and rising from the dead.

Here is a summary of the conclusions Strobel made in his book that caused him to abandon his atheistic lifestyle in order to follow the truth:

1) Jesus' biographies have been reliably preserved for us: Strobel says that world-class scholar on the subject, Bruce Metzger, concludes that "compared with other ancient documents, there is an unprecedented number of New Testament manuscripts and they can be dated extremely close to the original writing." (p. 350)

2) There is credible evidence for Jesus outside His biographies: "Sources from outside the Bible corroborate that many people believed Jesus performed healings and was the Messiah, that he was crucified, and that despite this shameful death, his followers, who believed he was still alive, worshipped him as God." (p.351)

3) Archeological evidence confirms what's written in Jesus' biographies: "No discovery has ever disproved a biblical reference." (p.351)

4) Jesus was really convinced that He was the Son of God: "Jesus had a supreme and transcendent self-understanding." (p.352)

5) Jesus fulfilled the attributes of God: "the New Testament specifically confirms that Jesus ultimately possessed every qualification of deity, including omniscience, omnipresence, omnipotence, eternality, and immutability." (p.353)

6) Jesus alone matched the identity of the Messiah: Jesus fulfilled all the Old Testament prophecies that were written about the coming Messiah. "Against astronomical odds—one chance in a trillion, trillion, trillion, trillion, trillion, trillion, trillion, trillion, trillion, trillion, trillion, trillion, trillion—Jesus and only Jesus throughout history, matched this prophetic fingerprint." (p. 354)

7) *Jesus' body was really absent from His tomb*: "In fact nobody, not even the Roman soldiers or Jewish leaders, ever claimed that the tomb still contained Jesus' body." (p. 355)

8) *Jesus was seen alive after His death on the cross*: Over five hundred witnesses saw Jesus alive after His resurrection. "Concluded British theologian Michael Green, 'The appearances of Jesus are as well authenticated as anything in antiquity…There can be no rational doubt that they occurred.'" (p.355)

9) *There are supporting facts that point to the Resurrection*: It is highly unlikely that *every* apostle would have "knowingly and willingly" gone to their deaths for a lie. Some may go to their deaths firmly believing something that is false, but the disciples were in the unique historical position of *knowing* firsthand that Jesus Christ had risen from the dead.

Also, it's hard to imagine the conversion of known skeptics like Paul and James and the mass conversions of thousands of other Jews to this new religion. The church's early sacraments of baptism and communion "affirmed Jesus' resurrection and deity." Finally, "the miraculous emergence of the church in the face of brutal Roman persecution 'rips a great hole in history, a hole the size and shape of resurrection,' as C.F.D. Moule put it." (p.356)

With the very high standards for acceptance in the final canon of Scripture we know as the Bible and the incredible historical, archeological, and prophetic accuracy of these writings, we must conclude that the Bible is clearly more than just a collection of books written by forty different human authors.

For Christians of all denominations, we have very sound reasons for putting our faith in the contents of this Book and believing it is divinely inspired and clearly the standard by which doctrines of our faith must be judged.

We also know that the Bible has stood the test of time. Some books of the Bible have been in existence for close to four thousand years. The books of the New Testament have been in existence for nearly two thousand years.

These writings have withstood the persecutions of the Roman Empire, which sought to wipe out Christianity, as well as many other hostile regimes throughout the centuries.

The Bible has also stood the test of criticism by human authors attempting to discredit it. The latest example is Dan Brown's *The DaVinci Code*. This book is full of false allegations about the Bible and church history. It has sold millions of copies and caused many to question what they believe about Christianity. Despite Brown's incredible success with this book, a thousand years from now, the Bible will still be standing tall while *The DaVinci Code* will be in the ash heap of history.

In the final analysis, we Christians can trust that the Bible is God's inspired Word because we know that God not only wrote it (through human authors), but also guarded it through the ages so that we, His people, would always have it as the standard for how we should live and what we must do to obtain eternal salvation.

3. Does the Bible have total doctrinal authority or can the Catholic Church make a proclamation that is contrary to it?

From the Catholic Church's standpoint, this is clearly the most controversial of the three questions. After all, the Church claims to have been the guardians of the faith for almost two thousand years. The early Church councils assembled the Bible into its present form.

Some may argue that the Church has been given divine authority to decide what is and isn't part of official Christian doctrine. In recent centuries, many popes have claimed their proclamations are "infallible."

There are five main criteria that have been established in order for a Church doctrine to be considered "infallible." These five were established at the First Vatican Council in 1868 and reaffirmed at the Second Vatican Council in 1963. They are as follows:

1) The doctrine must be issued directly by the office and person of the pope.
2) The doctrine must be issued "in virtue of his office, when as the supreme shepherd and teacher of all the faithful, who confirms his brethren in their faith" (Catechism 891). In other words, while conducting his official duties as pope.
3) The pope must make a definitive proclamation of this doctrine.
4) "A doctrine of faith or morals" ("And this infallibility...in defining doctrine of faith and morals, extends as far as the deposit of revelation extends").
5) The doctrine is universal, and it is the requirement of the entire Church to accept and believe this doctrine.

While Church doctrine needs to be highly respected, especially if it comes directly from the pope, can they ever really claim a doctrine to be infallible? Sacred Church tradition should be given a lot of credence and held in high regard, but should it be placed on the same level as Scripture?

Since tradition could never meet the incredibly stringent litmus tests that a writing had to meet to become part of Scripture, the answer to that question must be no.

And what about the Church's "infallible" proclamations? At times throughout Church history, the pope has made proclamations of infallibility of a particular doctrine. This is usually done after a long succession of popes have affirmed this doctrine to be true.

With all due respect to Church authority, this practice seems to be quite dangerous. How can human beings, even popes, ever claim that their proclamations are infallible? *Only* God is infallible. *Only* God's words can be infallible. We know that the Bible is divinely inspired because of the criteria we previously discussed for its assembly, but how can we know that Church proclamations are divinely inspired, and thus infallible?

Just because three or four or five consecutive popes affirm something to be true does not make it true. Although most of these popes have been holy men of God and highly knowledgeable about God's ways, history has shown that they are all capable of making mistakes.

Even the apostle Paul admitted that he made mistakes and did not have a monopoly on the truth. Paul says in 1 Corinthians 13:12, "now we see but a poor reflection as in a mirror; then we shall see face to face. Now I know in part, then I shall know fully, even as I am fully known." The *then* Paul is talking about is after he dies.

Paul was humble enough to admit that he couldn't possibly have a perfect understanding of the ways of God until he reached heaven. You wouldn't have found even the most accomplished of popes claim that he is holier or more spiritual than the apostle Paul.

The Catholic Church has also shown by its actions throughout the centuries that it is far from infallible. This is a sensitive issue for millions of loyal Catholics who believe the Church is always right, but unfortunately the facts of history speak for themselves.

From the Crusades to the Spanish Inquisition to the burning at the stake of St Joan of Arc, to countless other examples, the Church has proven its actions were not divinely inspired at times. Most notable among these was the excommunication of Martin Luther that led to the Protestant Reformation.

Martin Luther definitely had many flaws, but his opposition to Rome was warranted. The Catholic Church had become so corrupt that they were actually in the practice of selling indulgences. In effect, the salvation of your soul and entry into heaven was available at the right price. All you had to do to get a relative out of purgatory was give enough gold to the Church. All you needed to do to assure your own salvation was give enough gold to the Church.

This was the height of corruption. Because so few people at the time could read and the Bible wasn't translated into many of the common languages, the Church was the main gatekeeper of the truth.

Very few people could check what Church leaders were saying against Scripture because most common people couldn't read Scripture. Therefore, they trusted what the Church told them. This kind of unaccountable doctrinal authority in the hands of fallible human beings was a recipe for disaster.

The disaster in this case was the fact that the Catholic Church violated the trust of millions of members who put their faith in the Church to give them the truth about their salvation. Many millions of souls were probably led astray because of their blind trust in Church doctrine at that time.

These examples show that the Catholic Church is a fallible human institution with some corruption in its history. Now the Church has also done many great and noble acts throughout the centuries.

The previous examples were not cited to focus on the negative aspects of the Church. They were cited to simply make the point that it is absurd to think the Church can credibly make any proclamation of infallibility.

Since the evidence strongly suggests the Bible is truly divinely inspired and the Catholic Church is a God-ordained institution that is definitely capable of making mistakes, it is only logical to conclude that Scripture has total authority when it comes to answering questions about God's plan for salvation.

The Church can certainly supplement what's already written in Scripture, as they do with the Catechism, but it is probable that even most Catholics would agree the Church cannot directly contradict what's written in the Bible.

CHAPTER 2

The Church's Official Positions on Sacred Scripture and Mary

In order to get to the real truth about what may be wrong with the Catholic Church's doctrine on the Virgin Mary and whether or not it contradicts the Bible, we must first find out what the Church's *actual* positions are on the Scriptures and Mary.

There are many misconceptions among non-Catholics and Catholics about where the church stands on these issues. The best place to go to find out the truth is *The Catechism of the Catholic Church*.

The Catechism of the Catholic Church is like a supplement to the Bible that contains more than nine hundred pages of Catholic doctrine. It has been revised over the centuries and was last updated by Pope John Paul II in 1992. The Catechism is *the* source for Church doctrine on almost any subject, and it has a lot to say about the Scriptures and the Virgin Mary.

The Church's Position on Scripture

This may surprise many non-Catholics, but the Catholic Church actually *does* believe that the Bible is the inerrant word of God. Consider these passages from the Catechism:

Catechism 104: "In Sacred Scripture, the Church constantly finds her nourishment and her strength, for she welcomes it not as a human word, 'but as what it really is, the word of God.' 'In the sacred books, the Father who is in Heaven comes lovingly to meet his children, and talks with them.'"

Catechism 133: "The Church 'forcefully and specifically exhorts all the Christian faithful…to learn the surpassing knowledge of Jesus Christ, by frequent reading of the divine Scriptures. Ignorance of the Scriptures is ignorance of Christ.'"

Catechism 136: "God is the author of Sacred Scripture because he inspired its human authors; he acts in them and by means of them. He thus gives assurance that their writings teach without error his saving truth."

These passages show that the Church clearly believes the Scriptures are divinely inspired. Not only are they considered divinely inspired, they are considered essential for the Christian to receive God's spoken Word and to become intimately familiar with Jesus Christ, the center of our faith. In the church's view, not knowing the Scriptures is equivalent to not knowing Christ Himself.

The above description of the Catholic Church's view of Scripture would probably be the view of most other Christians. The major area of disagreement with other Christian denominations would be the Church's view of the relationship between sacred Scripture, sacred Church tradition and the Magisterium of the Church.

Although the Church believes that Scripture is without question the inspired Word of God, it also believes that its sacred traditions (throughout the centuries following Christ's resurrection) and the interpretations of sacred Scripture and sacred tradition by the pope and his high ranking bishops are equally divinely inspired and carry the same weight as sacred Scripture itself. Catechism 95 summarizes this view:

> It is clear therefore that, in the supremely wise arrangement of God, sacred Tradition, Sacred Scripture, and the Magisterium of the Church are so connected and associated that one of them cannot stand without the others. Working together, each in its own way, under the action of one Holy Spirit, they all contribute effectively to the salvation of souls.

This is where the Church seems to go astray. It doesn't seem credible to put traditions and papal doctrines developed centuries after Christ on the same level as sacred Scripture, written within a generation of Christ's death and resurrection.

It is also hard to believe that *only* the pope and top-level bishops have the authority to correctly interpret Scripture. This seems like a doctrine that's left over from the middle ages, when the Bible was only available in a few languages and most common people couldn't read it for themselves.

At that time, others couldn't interpret Scripture because they didn't have access to it. People had to trust what their priests told them because there was no way they could verify it for themselves.

When Church officials had exclusive access to Scripture, did they act as responsible guardians of the faith? Unfortunately, the facts of history show otherwise.

Although most non-Catholics wouldn't agree with the Church's position on tradition and papal proclamations as they relate to Scripture, there seems to be enough common ground with regard to the supremacy of Scripture to find some agreement on these issues.

The bottom line is that we, as Christians, can all agree that the Bible is the divinely inspired Word of God. If it is the Word of God and is without error, then, no matter what else the Church says, it is not possible for any true Christian doctrine to be contradictory to the Bible.

The Church's Position on the Virgin Mary

The Catholic Church holds the Virgin Mary in the highest regard. Only God Himself, along with His Son Jesus Christ and the Holy Spirit, are viewed more favorably. The Church has many names for her and many doctrines concerning her.

Also, because the Catholic Church has approximately 1.1 billion people living in almost every region on the planet, there are obviously many varying opinions of what Mary's true role in the Church should be. In this book, we are going to focus mainly on the Church's "official" position taken from the *Catechism of the Catholic Church*.

According to Catechism 148, "The Virgin Mary most perfectly embodies the obedience of faith." These are the first words written about Mary in the Catechism. The first thing the Church says about her is that she is the most perfect model of our faith.

She is *the* role model and standard for how we as Christians should view our faith. She didn't just believe in God, she was obedient to Him in the greatest task a human being has ever been commissioned to perform—to give birth to the Savior of the world, raise Him, and be faithful to Him all the way to His death on the cross.

If you think about it, her task must have seemed more than overwhelming. First, to be told that she is pregnant with a child by the Holy Spirit, then to have to convince her future husband Joseph that this was true. She must have had to endure great shame from a society that probably believed this child was born out of wedlock.

After Jesus' birth, she faced the pressure of having to raise the child she knew would grow up to be the Messiah. She may not have known what exactly that would look like, but she knew that Jesus was destined for greatness. Finally, to see it all seemingly come crashing down and being powerless to do anything about it as she watched Jesus die the most brutal death imaginable on the cross.

Through all these hardships and the ultimate triumph of Christ's resurrection, Mary never wavered in her faith. She remained God's humble, faithful, and obedient servant all the days that she walked this earth. If Abraham is the father of our faith, Mary is definitely the mother of our faith.

Another Church doctrine concerning Mary is that she was immaculately conceived and lived a sinless life. Although it emerged gradually throughout the centuries, this doctrine was finally made official by Pope Pius IX in 1854.

Catechism 490 partially explains why it was necessary for the Church to develop this doctrine: "in order for Mary to be able to give the free assent of her faith to the announcement of her vocation, it was necessary that she be wholly borne of God's grace."

In other words, Mary was preserved free from the stain of original sin because this condition was necessary for her to give birth to Jesus Christ, who was God in human form. The Scripture used to support this doctrine is Luke 1:28, where the angel Gabriel greets Mary with the words, "hail, full of grace! The Lord is with you." The words "full of grace" are taken to mean without sin.

It should be noted here that there is definitely dispute about whether or not those words truly imply that Mary was without sin. Most translations of the Bible use different words for this exchange.

For example, the Catholic Church approved Jerusalem Bible translates Luke 1:28 as "Rejoice, so highly favored!

The Lord is with you." We'll explore this controversy in further detail in Chapter 4.

From the earliest centuries of Church history, Mary has been thought of as "ever-virgin." Catechism 506 explains some of the reasoning behind this doctrine: "Mary is a virgin because her virginity is *the sign of her faith* 'unadulterated by any doubt,' and of her undivided gift of herself to God's will." This belief was made official Catholic dogma in 553 A.D. by the Second Council of Constantinople.

In 431 A.D., the council of Ephesus gave the Church another doctrine concerning Mary. They declared her "Mother of God." This declaration was made in response to the Nestorian heresy that was popular at the time.

The Nestorian heresy denied that Jesus Christ was God. The proclamation that Mary is "Mother of God" sought to reaffirm and solidify the Church's already established doctrine that Jesus Christ was and is truly God in human form.

The declaration of Mary as the Mother of God opened up the door for Mary's ever-expansive role in the Catholic Church. Since that time, she has taken on many official and unofficial titles and roles in the Church. For example, if Mary is "Mother of God," it is very easy to view her as the mother of God's church.

Other titles that have followed include "Advocate," "Helper," "Benefactress," and perhaps the most controversial official doctrine of "Mediatrix." Catechism 969 helps explain this progression:

> This motherhood of Mary in the order of grace continues uninterruptedly from the consent which she loyally gave at the Annunciation and which she sustained without wavering beneath the cross, until the eternal fulfillment of all the elect. Taken up to heaven she did not lay aside this saving office but by

her manifold intercession continues to bring us gifts of eternal salvation…Therefore the Blessed Virgin is invoked in the Church under the titles of Advocate, Helper, Benefactress, and Mediatrix.

The belief in Mary as "Mediatrix" of all graces has serious implications. It implies that mankind cannot receive any grace from God unless it comes through Mary. This is the primary reason why millions of Catholics say prayers to Mary daily. This is also the primary reason why most Protestants are opposed to the Catholic Church's view of Mary's role in salvation.

After all, if the only way to obtain grace from God is through Mary, and most Protestant churches don't believe in praying to Mary, then the implied conclusion is that, according to the Catholic Church, most Protestant denominations are unable to receive God's grace.

There are two other doctrines worth mentioning concerning Mary that are widely held beliefs within the Church. The first is that Mary was assumed into heaven and crowned Queen of heaven and earth. The second is that Mary is *Coredemptrix* with Christ in the salvation of mankind.

Mary's title of *Queen of heaven* dates back to the seventh century A.D. Although I could not locate the term in the official Catechism, it has been used by various popes throughout the centuries. This is another title that seems to have stemmed from the *Mother of God* title in the fifth century.

As mentioned earlier, if she is indeed *Mother of God*, then she becomes part of the royal bloodline. It naturally follows that she could be considered *Queen of heaven.*

The *Coredemptrix* title has been in use for about six hundred years. Although this title is also not found in the Catechism, the description of it is laid out in Catechism 494: "As St Irenaeus says, 'Being obedient she became the cause of salvation for herself and for the whole human race.'…

'what the virgin Eve bound through her disbelief, Mary loosened by her faith.'"

In other words, because of Mary's cooperation in giving birth to and raising Christ our Redeemer, she "became the cause" of her own salvation and the salvation of the entire human race. If Mary is indeed the cause of her own and our salvation, she would be worthy of the title of *Coredemptrix*.

This final doctrine of *Coredemptrix* is the most controversial and has yet to be declared official Catholic dogma. There has been a movement underway since the late '90s by many prominent Church leaders to make this dogma official. So far, the Vatican has not given any indication that it will take such an action.

This is by no means an exhaustive list of the Catholic Church's positions on sacred Scripture or the titles and roles that Mary has been given by the Church throughout the last two thousand years. However, these are the core beliefs of the Church, taken directly from the *Catechism of the Catholic Church* and other official church sources. Discussion of these doctrines and their implications on our own salvation will be the focus of the remaining chapters of this book.

CHAPTER 3

Mary: The Perfect Realization of the Faith

The Catholic Church rightly gives the Virgin Mary the highest honors that any saint could possibly receive. They venerate her as the "perfect realization" of the Christian faith. The Church holds that Mary was faithful and obedient to God's calling on her life and proceeded to cooperate in the single greatest act of human service: giving birth to and raising our Lord and Savior, Jesus Christ. This makes Mary the ultimate role model, not only for mothers, but for all people.

The Virgin Mary was just a teenager when God called her to this very special life. The visit from the angel Gabriel greatly troubled her. Naturally, she questioned how it would be possible for her to bear a child while still being a virgin. After Gabriel explained the situation to her, she simply responded, "I am the Lord's servant…may it be to me as you have said." (Luke 1:38)

While some may take for granted Mary's favorable response to the angel, let's contrast this with the response of Zechariah earlier in the first chapter of Luke. Zechariah was Elizabeth's husband, making her Mary's cousin-in-law. He was a descendant of Aaron and a holy priest. The text also states that Zechariah and Elizabeth were "upright in the sight of God, observing all the Lord's commandments and regulations blamelessly" (Luke 1:6).

Zechariah definitely was a religious and spiritual man. He knew all the laws and customs and observed them as well as he possibly could. This man was more upright than probably ninety-nine percent of the people of his time or any other time.

Despite all of this, when the angel Gabriel appeared to Zechariah and told him that God had answered his prayers and his wife would have a child in her old age, Zechariah did not believe. Consequently, he was not allowed to speak until the event finally occurred.

Before we condemn Zechariah, we must remember that most of us would have reacted exactly the same way. Think about it. If your wife was more than sixty years old, had never had children, and you were told by an angel of the Lord that she was going to have a child, would you believe it? First of all, you'd probably seriously question whether or not you were hallucinating or where the vision was coming from.

Ladies, imagine that you are a teenager, have never been with a man, and are told by an angel of the Lord that you are going to have a son. When you ask how this is possible, you are told that the Holy Spirit will come upon you and overshadow you. You've never heard of a virgin birth in all of previous human history. How would you react to such news?

I think the answer is that 99.9 percent of women would react the way Zechariah did. Even if they were blameless and upright, they'd still probably react like Zechariah. They'd seriously question the angel and wonder if they weren't losing their mind. This is what makes Mary's act of faith so special.

Mary was no priest in the temple. Although she was familiar with Jewish Scripture and law, she didn't have anywhere near the depth of knowledge possessed by Zechariah. She was just a simple, insignificant peasant girl from an insignificant town in an insignificant Roman province of Judea. The only special thing she did was to say yes to God.

The child-like faith Mary displayed in saying yes to God caused her to become blessed among all women. This is the kind of faith that each of us, as Christians, should be trying to imitate. If we could only say yes to God with the childlike faith Mary had, think of all the wonderful things God could accomplish through us!

Catechism 148 explains the Catholic Church's view on Mary's great faithfulness: "The Virgin Mary most perfectly embodies the obedience of faith. Mary welcomes the tidings and promise brought by the angel Gabriel, believing that 'with God nothing will be impossible' and so giving her assent: 'behold I am the handmaid of the Lord; let it be [done] to me according to your word.'"

Catechism 149 continues:

"Throughout her life and until her last ordeal when Jesus her son died on the cross, Mary's faith never wavered. She never ceased to believe in the fulfillment of God's word. And so the Church venerates in Mary the purest realization of faith."

Unfortunately, this deep respect and veneration for the blessed mother is unique to the Catholic and Orthodox Churches. For two thousand years, these churches have been faithful in their duty to give Mary the honor and respect she deserves. They have fulfilled Mary's own prophesy during her joyful song when she says "all generations will call me blessed."(Luke 1:48)

Many of the Protestant churches, by contrast, seem to go out of their way to avoid giving Mary any kind of mention. Every Mother's Day, Protestant pastors give sermons praising many of the famous biblical mothers as great role models. Very seldom do these pastors talk about the blessed mother of Jesus.

If Sarah, Rebecca, Rachel, and Ruth are worthy of hailing as great biblical role models for mothers of today, why do they so seldom mention Mary? Are Mary's unequalled obedience, faith, and self-sacrifice unworthy of discussion in today's mostly self-centered society? Does she have nothing to teach us today about being better Christians?

It is true that a good part of the Protestant resistance to discussing Mary has to do with their belief that the Catholic Church has idolized Mary to the point of breaking the First Commandment. Even if that were true, would that justify failing to give Mary the respect she deserves?

Let's put this another way. Most Protestants believe in a literal interpretation of the Scripture. Scripture records Mary prophesying that "every generation will call me blessed." *Every* generation includes *our* present generation. Therefore, God commands *our* generation to call her blessed.

What does it really mean to honor Mary by calling her blessed? God didn't write this story through Luke just to record history. Yes, Mary was a great woman and a great saint that displayed more faith and obedience than perhaps any other human being in history. We don't read about it just to marvel at what great faith she had. We read about it so we can be encouraged to try to develop faith like hers.

The exciting thing is that if we say yes to God with the same childlike faith Mary had, the blessings we receive from God will be similar to those bestowed upon Mary. This is God's promise to all His children. No matter how old we are or how many times we've failed in the past, it's never too late to say yes to God and enter His promised land for our lives.

CHAPTER 4

The Immaculate Conception

Very few people would dispute the idea that Mary was a woman of incredible faith. Even though Protestant teachers often fail to emphasize this fact, they almost never dispute it. Mary's faith is definitely a doctrine that all of us as Christians can and should unite behind. The controversy begins with the Catholic Church's doctrine of the *Immaculate Conception*.

First we must clarify exactly what we are talking about. Many outside the Church hear the words *Immaculate Conception* and assume we are referring to the conception of Jesus Christ in Mary's womb by the Holy Spirit.

Although there is certainly agreement among Christians that Jesus was immaculately conceived, the Catholic Church is talking about the immaculate conception of the Virgin Mary.

As mentioned in chapter two, the Catholic Church's official dogma is that the Virgin Mary herself was conceived sinless in the womb of her mother Ann. They say that Mary was preserved without original sin for the purpose of carrying the Son of God into the world. This was supposedly necessary because God could not be carried inside an impure womb.

So did Mary really live a sinless life? If she did, she would be the exception to *every* other human being in history except Jesus Christ Himself. This would make Mary more than just the perfect role model of human faith, it would give her a distinction that no other human being could ever lay claim to: living a perfect and sin-free life.

So how does the Catholic Church arrive at its conclusion for her immaculate conception? Many in the Church argue that it would not be logically possible for God in human form to enter the womb of a sinner. They say God has nothing whatsoever to do with sin, so how could He have been born to a sinner? Sounds pretty logical, doesn't it?

The Church also backs this doctrine with four words of scriptural evidence from Luke 1:28: "hail, full of grace." The Church argues that these four words of Scripture clearly show that Mary was sinless. They say that *full* of grace means not lacking any grace.

If Mary doesn't lack any grace, then she must have had the perfect amount of grace needed to *never* commit a sin. On its surface, this again sounds like a pretty strong argument.

So let's look at the first argument for the *Immaculate Conception* of Mary: God could not enter the womb of a sinner. A valid response to this would be why not?

If God created the entire universe and everything in it by simply speaking a word, why couldn't He be born in the womb of a sinner? Also, if God could enter and live in a totally fallen and sinful world, then why couldn't He have been conceived in a sinner's womb?

It sounds like the Church is trying to use human logic to explain the ways of God. Now I'm not saying we shouldn't use our reasoning and logic to try to figure things out. God encourages us through the Proverbs and other places to gain wisdom and understanding. I'm simply saying that there are many mysteries of God that we will never understand on this side of heaven.

There are many examples of God's unsolved mysteries. Here are just a couple of them:

1) How do we logically explain why a perfectly loving God would allow terrible things to happen to good people?

2) Maybe a more important question is why would a perfectly loving God allow children of His to be created, *knowing* that many of them would reject Him and spend eternity in hell?

    People have been wrestling with and trying to reason their way through these questions for centuries. What usually ends up happening when we apply human logic to these difficult questions is that the person doing the reasoning either ends up denying God exists, rejecting God, or changing his/her image of God from the God of the Bible to a God that suits his/her purpose. This is clearly a dangerous road that leads us away from the truth.

    A better way to deal with these mysteries might be to apply Scripture instead of human logic to the ways of God. Scripture clearly says that God's ways are unexplainable. Isaiah 55:9 says, "as the heavens are higher than the earth so are my ways higher than your ways." This passage implies that God's ways are far above our own and can't totally be understood.

    Paul also contemplates the incredible, mysterious ways of God in Romans 11:33-34: "Oh, the depth of the riches of the wisdom of God! How unsearchable his judgments, and his paths beyond tracing out! Who has known the mind of the Lord? Or who has been his counselor?"

    Once again we find the apostle Paul, a great saint and man of incredible depth of understanding of the ways of God admitting that he doesn't see anywhere close to the full picture regarding the ways of God.

    Paul is essentially saying it is impossible for humans to figure God out. By making this admission, Paul stays clear of the dangerous road of trying to explain God's mysteries with human logic.

This brings us back to the Catholic Church's argument that God in human form couldn't have entered the womb of a sinner. If we wanted to further carry out this type of reasoning, wouldn't we then have to conclude that Mary's mother Ann must have had a purified womb in order to bring sinless Mary into the world?

And if Ann was sinless, wouldn't her mother have been sinless as well? And if her mother was sinless, her grandmother and great-grandmother must have also been sinless. You can see how silly this argument becomes. If we carry out this reasoning to its full conclusion, we would have to believe that everyone in Jesus' genealogy was sinless. We know that this was not the case.

If we want to still insist that God can't have anything to do with sin and therefore Jesus must have been carried in a purified womb, then why was Jesus brought into a sinful world? Jesus was raised by both Mary and Joseph, and we know that at least one of them was a sinner.

Jesus was raised and grew up among sinful people. All His family members were sinners, and everyone he came in contact with was a sinner. After Jesus began His ministry around age thirty, He made a regular practice of hanging around with some of the worst of sinners. These included tax collectors and prostitutes, the kind of people that were shunned by most of society.

Some of the apostles Jesus chose were from groups like these. Matthew was a tax collector, and Mary Magdalene was a woman with seven demons that Jesus cast out. We're not really sure what her story was, but she definitely had some serious issues. If God *can't* have anything to do with sin, why didn't Jesus go off into the desert by Himself and stay away from the sinful people inhabiting the world?

Finally, when Jesus died on the cross in our place, He *became* sin for us (2 Corinthians 5:21). That's right. The Bible teaches that Jesus died in our place and took the punishment for all the sins of the world with His death on the cross. The bottom line is if God *can't* have anything to do with sin, then why did God send His only Son to earth to redeem a sinful world? I guess we have to chalk that one up as another of the great mysteries of God.

Now let's look at the Church's scriptural backing for the doctrine of Mary's *Immaculate Conception*. This backing consists of four words from Luke 1:28: "hail, full of grace." These were the words spoken to Mary by the angel Gabriel when he visited her in an event known as the *Annunciation*. Does this greeting by the angel Gabriel really indicate that Mary was without sin? The Catholic Church certainly believes this to be the case.

On the surface, their argument appears to have merit. You can easily argue that "full" in this context means not lacking any, hence making Mary as graceful as possible. Furthermore, since Luke did not explain further what Gabriel was really trying to say, the passage was left open to interpretation.

There is one problem with the Catholic Church's interpretation of this verse. It is that not all versions of the Bible translate Luke 1:28 as "hail, full of grace." Many newer versions of the Bible translate the passage as "greetings, you who are highly favored," or similar wording. Even The Jerusalem Bible and some other Catholic Church approved translations use this wording.

Obviously, the latter scriptural translations using the words "highly favored" to describe Mary's status would strongly argue against her being without sin. In fact, it would seem that she was simply one of the most blessed of God's creatures without saying that she was sinless.

In order to discover if the Church's argument is meritorious, we must figure out which translation is most accurate. To accomplish this, we will look at the original Greek used by the author Luke. The Greek word used in Luke 1:28 is *kecharitomene*. The root of this word is *charito*.

The word *charito* can be found in Ephesians 1:6. In this context, Paul is describing God's glorious grace, freely given to us (all believers). Clearly, Paul is not saying that we as believers are perfect or sinless; he is saying that we are freely receiving God's grace because of our faith in Christ. This would imply that we, as believers, are "highly favored" by virtue of receiving God's grace.

Given the serious doubts about which translation is most accurate for Luke 1:28, it would seem that the Church's use of it to support the *Immaculate Conception* doctrine is not warranted. There really is no other supporting Scripture to clarify this passage, so the only other thing to look at in Scripture is whether or not this principle is supported.

Is it possible for a human being other than God (Jesus Christ) to be without sin? Of course, with God, all things are possible. As I said earlier in this chapter, God created the universe and set up the rules, so He could certainly have preserved one human being from ever sinning.

The challenge with this argument is if you believe that sacred Scripture is God-breathed, then you *must* not contradict it. When we look at sacred Scripture for any precedent of a human being other than Christ being sinless, we find none. There were many that were most righteous, such as Enoch, Job, Abraham, Joseph and others, but none that were clearly shown to be sinless.

On the other hand, there are several passages of Scripture that tell us we are all sinners. The clearest passage on this subject is Romans 3:23: "All have sinned and fall short of the glory of God." Paul was a contemporary of Mary and probably wrote the book of Romans during her lifetime or shortly thereafter. Had Mary been without sin, Paul probably would have known this and written about it.

In the book of Romans, Paul gives us a very comprehensive description of the doctrine of justification by grace through faith in Jesus Christ. If you read through this book, you'll find throughout that it is all-inclusive. Paul is not leaving anyone out here.

"First for the Jew, then for the Gentile" is an often repeated phrase in this book. If Mary was the one exception to this rule, it's probable that Paul or one of the other New Testament writers would have made it clear for all of us to know.

Mary's own words also imply she was a fallen creature. In Luke 1:46-47 she says "my soul glorifies the Lord and my spirit rejoices in God my *savior*." Now why would a person without sin need a savior? If she were without sin, she would not have needed Jesus to shed His blood for her.

The bottom line is that the Catholic Church's doctrine of Mary's *Immaculate Conception* is contradictory to sacred Scripture. No matter how it is explained or justified, there is no getting around this fact.

The Bible clearly states in many different parts that every human being except Jesus Christ is guilty of sin. There are no exceptions to this rule in the Old or the New Testament. Finally, Mary herself acknowledges her sinfulness by acknowledging the need for a savior.

CHAPTER 5

Mary's Perpetual Virginity and Assumption

Another controversial Church doctrine that is closely related to the *Immaculate Conception* is the belief that Mary was a perpetual virgin. In other words, she remained a virgin her entire life. This doctrine has been popular since the earliest days of the Church and was made official dogma at the Second Council of Constantinople in 553 A.D.

The reasoning for this doctrine is if Mary was sinless and pure in carrying Jesus, her womb must have been preserved sinless and pure after Jesus' birth.

Catechism 499 explains it this way; "In fact, Christ's birth 'did not diminish his mother's virginal integrity but sanctified it.' And so the liturgy of the Church celebrates Mary as *Aeiparthenos*, the 'Ever-virgin.'" It appears the Church is saying that after perfection in the form of Christ had been in her womb, nothing imperfect could ever enter it again.

This is another case of applying human logic to a godly mystery. The precedent for this kind of reasoning was already set with the *Immaculate Conception* doctrine, so it was easy to follow with the *Perpetual Virginity* doctrine.

The *Perpetual Virginity* doctrine is far less controversial than the *Immaculate Conception* doctrine as it does not violate any scriptural principles. In fact, it is entirely plausible that Mary could have remained a virgin her entire life. The problem with this doctrine is that the New Testament seems to indicate that Jesus did have brothers and sisters.

Jesus' siblings are first mentioned when Jesus was visiting his hometown in Matthew 13:55-56: "Isn't this the carpenter's son? Isn't his mother's name Mary, and aren't his brothers James, Joseph, Simon and Judas? Aren't all his sisters with us?" Mark 6:3 is essentially the same passage as Matthew 13:55-56. Both name Jesus' brothers and indicate that he had sisters as well.

Luke 8:20 is another passage that mentions Jesus' mother and brothers. "Someone told him (Jesus) 'your mother and brothers are standing outside, wanting to see you.'" Jesus went on to explain that His real mother and brothers were those who hear God's Word and put it into practice.

Apparently, the early Church also believed that Jesus had siblings because the apostle Paul referred to James as the Lord's brother (Gal 1:19). Surely Paul would not have given James that title if he weren't at the very least a close relative of the Lord.

Assuming we believe sacred Scripture, there are really only three possible explanations for these passages:

1) These siblings of Jesus were stepchildren of Joseph by a previous wife that maybe died before he met Mary.

2) They were actually cousins or close relations of Jesus and therefore were not the Virgin Mary's children.

3) These were actually Jesus' brothers and sisters and children of Mary, thereby invalidating the Church's *Perpetual Virginity* doctrine.

The first possible scenario—the siblings of Jesus mentioned in the New Testament were stepchildren of Joseph—is highly unlikely. The primary reason is that they aren't mentioned during the time period before Christ's birth.

For example, if Jesus' brothers and sisters were Joseph's children from a previous wife, then where were they when Mary and Joseph were traveling to Bethlehem to give birth to Jesus? Also, they are not mentioned during Mary and Joseph's time living in Egypt. Finally, the Catholic Church has never officially endorsed this theory, so it is probably the least likely of the three.

The second scenario that Jesus' siblings mentioned in the New Testament were actually his cousins is closest to the official Church explanation. Here is what the Church says from Catechism 500:

> Against this doctrine (Perpetual Virginity) the objection is sometimes raised that the Bible mentions brothers and sisters of Jesus. The Church has always understood these passages as not referring to other children of the Virgin Mary. In fact James and Joseph, 'brothers of Jesus,' are the sons of another Mary, a disciple of Christ, whom St Matthew significantly calls 'the other Mary.' They are close relations of Jesus, according to an Old Testament expression.

In the Catechism, the Church doesn't really say if "the other Mary" is a relative of Jesus, only that they are "close relations...according to an Old Testament expression," whatever that means. In any case, the Church is referring to Matthew's mention of "the other Mary" in Matthew 27:61. Earlier in Matthew 27:56, he refers to her as "Mary the mother of James and Joses."

The "other Mary" mentioned by Matthew is probably the same Mary identified in John 19:25 as "his mother's sister, Mary the wife of Clopas." These are the only passages where this "other Mary" is mentioned, so we wouldn't exactly call her role "significant." She is, however, identified as the Virgin Mary's sister and the mother of James and Joses, two people close to Jesus.

There were three significant people named James in the early Church. One is the brother of John and one of the inner circle of Jesus' disciples. The second is James, son of Alphaeus, identified in three of the Gospels as one of the disciples. Very little else is known about this James. The third James is the one known by the early church as the brother of the Lord and believed to have written the New Testament book of James.

It is unclear from these passages in Matthew and John who this "other Mary" really is and which James she is the mother of. Since the "other Mary" is not mentioned anywhere else, we will never really know the answer to these questions.

Even though this "other Mary" seems to be not only the Virgin Mary's sister but also the mother of two people named James and Joses, it doesn't prove that The Virgin Mary herself didn't have other children.

One reason it would seem likely that the Virgin Mary had other children is the aforementioned passage from Luke 8:20 (also referenced in Mark 3:31). If Jesus' mother was outside waiting for Him with his brothers, then where was this "other Mary?"

If these "brothers" were just cousins or close relations, then why isn't it the "other Mary" and not Jesus' mother traveling with them? This "other Mary" must have still been alive because she appears at the time of Jesus' death, so it would stand to reason that she would be the one traveling with her children, not Jesus' mother.

The conclusion of the matter is that we will never have irrefutable evidence either way. It seems most likely that scenario three is correct and that Jesus had actual brothers and sisters. The multiple New Testament references to these siblings make this the most plausible scenario.

The second scenario—these siblings were really Jesus' cousins—is also very possible. As mentioned earlier, if Mary were an "ever-virgin," that would certainly not violate any biblical principles. In fact, it would bolster the Church's claim that she was most holy and blessed among women. There just doesn't seem to be much evidence supporting this scenario.

The challenge for the Church is that, whatever the scriptural evidence, they absolutely can't accept the idea of Jesus having siblings and still have a *Perpetual Virginity* doctrine.

Also, If Mary had other children, their *Immaculate Conception* doctrine would collapse because there would have been imperfection inside Mary's womb. Therefore, the Church has no choice but to buy into the questionable scenario that Jesus had no direct siblings, just cousins or close relations, regardless of the biblical evidence to the contrary.

The Assumption of Mary

Following the *Immaculate Conception* and *Perpetual Virginity* doctrines is the *Assumption of Mary*. Since the 500s A.D., the Church has celebrated the feast of this *Assumption* on August 15.

In 1950, Pope Pius XII declared the *Assumption* official Catholic dogma with these words:

> "We pronounce, declare, and define it to be a divinely revealed dogma: that the Immaculate Mother of God, the ever Virgin Mary, having completed the course

of her earthly life, was assumed body and soul into heavenly glory."

Catechism 966 describes her assumption this way:

"Finally the Immaculate Virgin, preserved free from all stain of original sin, when the course of her earthly life was finished, was taken up body and soul into heavenly glory, and exalted by the Lord as Queen over all things, so that she might be the more fully conformed to her Son, the Lord of lords and conqueror of sin and death."

We're not going to spend a lot of time discussing this doctrine, mainly because there isn't a lot of support for it except for the usual human logic and reasoning used by the Church.

Almost nothing is said about Mary's life after Christ's resurrection in either the Bible or Church tradition. This doctrine is based almost entirely on the argument that since it was proper for God to do this, He must have done it.

In the New Testament, the Virgin Mary never appears after the four Gospels. We know from John 19:26-27 that Jesus entrusted the apostle John with the care of his mother and vice versa. After that, Mary is never again mentioned by name in the New Testament.

Church tradition also says very little about Mary's role in the early Church. Catechism 965 says that Mary "aided the beginnings of the Church by her prayers." Other than that, the Church is rather silent about the details surrounding Mary's life after Jesus' resurrection and ascension.

It is quite reasonable to believe that Mary remained a close confidant of the apostles during the early days of the Church. It is very likely that she was a source for Luke when he wrote his gospel in around the '50s A.D. Much of Luke's material about Mary could probably only have been obtained directly from Mary or someone close to her.

It is also very likely that Mary remained very close to John. Since Jesus entrusted them to each other, they would have been doing His explicit will to remain close to each other.

If Mary's assumption did indeed occur as the Church says, one might find it interesting that John did not mention it in his writings. Many scholars believe the Gospel of John was written around the year 90 A.D. Others believe it was written around 70 A.D.

In either case, if Mary was around fifteen or sixteen years old at the time of Jesus' birth, she would have been between 85 and 105 when John wrote his gospel. If Mary had been assumed to heaven, it seems likely that John would have known and written about it.

John did write one letter that could have been addressed to Mary. 2 John 1:1 says, "To the chosen lady and her children, whom I love in the truth…" Even though Mary was definitely a "chosen lady," the Catholic Church could never say this letter was meant for the Virgin Mary because it mentions the lady's children.

Later in the letter, John mentions having great joy at finding some of her children walking in the truth. This would imply that John is referring to specific physical children of this particular lady. If this lady had physical children, the Church would say that John *couldn't* have been writing to the Virgin Mary.

In any case, there is very little else we know about Mary's life after Christ's resurrection. So why does the Church hold as official dogma that Mary was assumed into heaven? The answer is that it must have happened because Mary was without sin.

If Mary was without sin, then she must not have experienced the ultimate wage of sin, which is death. Instead, God must have assumed her to heaven to sit with Jesus at the right hand of God.

As with the *Perpetual Virginity* doctrine, there is nothing in the Bible that would preclude the *Assumption* from happening. In fact, there is biblical precedent in the Old Testament for an assumption.

Both Enoch and Elijah were assumed into heaven and never experienced death, even though they were both human beings and neither of them were without sin.

The problem again is that the Church is making a proclamation without any scriptural (or traditional) evidence to back it up. The only support for this doctrine is flawed human logic: Because Mary was sinless, she must not have tasted death.

In fact, since two righteous yet sinful human beings from the Old Testament were assumed to heaven, it wouldn't make sense for the only non-divine sinless human being in history to experience death.

This again is flawed logic because of reasons earlier stated. God makes it clear in Isaiah 55:9 that "my ways are above your ways." Though God gave us intelligence and wisdom and a drive to understand His ways, there are certain things that will always remain a mystery.

Even if the Catholic Church's *Immaculate Conception* doctrine is valid and the Virgin Mary lived a sinless life, there is no reason why that would preclude her from dying. Jesus Himself was known to be without sin, yet He experienced a very brutal death.

The bottom line is that, because we have no evidence either way, no one really knows how Mary's life on earth ended. The Church doctrine that she was assumed to heaven is nothing more than an educated guess based on flawed human logic.

CHAPTER 6

Mary: "Mediatrix of all Graces"

The Catholic Church doctrines of Mary's *Immaculate Conception*, *Perpetual Virginity* and *Assumption* may be flawed, but in application they are fairly harmless. These doctrines only concern the person of Mary and nothing else. The problem is that they lead to a more dangerously flawed doctrine: Mary, *Mediatrix of all Graces*.

If we believe Mary was a sinless, ever-virgin who was assumed to heaven without experiencing death, this does not require us to change the way we relate to God or practice our Christian faith. Unfortunately, the Church doesn't stop there.

In proclaiming Mary *Mediatrix of all Graces*, they are saying that God's grace comes through Mary. Belief in this doctrine would require a radical change in the way we relate to God.

Here again is what the Catechism actually says regarding the *Mediatrix* doctrine:

> In a wholly singular way she cooperated by her obedience, faith, hope and burning charity in the Savior's work of restoring supernatural life to souls. For this reason she is a mother to us in the order of grace.

This motherhood of Mary in the order of grace continues uninterruptedly from the consent which she loyally gave at the Annunciation and which she sustained without wavering beneath the cross, until the eternal fulfillment of all the elect.

Taken up to heaven she did not lay aside this saving office but by her manifold intercession *continues to bring us gifts of eternal salvation*...Therefore the Blessed Virgin is invoked in the Church under the titles of Advocate, Helper, Benefactress, and *Mediatrix*.

Catechism 968-969

The Church is making a pretty big leap here. They seem to be saying that because Mary cooperated fully by being God's vehicle to bring the Savior into the world, Mary continues in this cooperation until all the elect are eternally fulfilled. What does Mary do in her continuance of this cooperation? She acts as our spiritual mother "in the order of grace."

Since Mary is considered the *Mediatrix of all Graces*, this would require a change in our behavior toward God. If Mary is in charge of dispensing all graces to the elect, then we would end up seeking grace through Mary and not through God. So we again go back to the question: where in Scripture do we find such a doctrine?

The short answer is we don't. The Virgin Mary is only mentioned a handful of times in Scripture and never in relation to obtaining God's grace. This is another doctrine that developed by tradition throughout the centuries and by various popes and other Church figures.

Also, we've established in chapter four that Mary was very likely a sinner like the rest of us. Nowhere in the Bible does it say otherwise, and it is well established in the Bible that all human beings are sinners, with Christ being the only exception.

If Mary was a sinner like the rest of us, then she was in just as much need of God's grace as anyone else. This would give us no reason to believe that she is now in charge of dispensing God's grace.

Let's explore some other biblical reasons why there are problems with the *Mediatrix* doctrine. If grace is indeed obtained through Mary, this goes against what we know and believe to be true about God in Scripture.

Paul gives an explanation of God's grace in Ephesians 1:6-8:

> To the praise of his glorious grace, which he has freely given us in the one (Jesus Christ) he loves. In him we have redemption through his blood, the forgiveness of sins, in accordance with the riches of God's grace that he lavished on us with all wisdom and understanding.

In this passage, Paul is saying that God has freely given us His grace in the *one* Jesus Christ. It's through *His* blood that we are redeemed and forgiven of our sins, and it is through *Him* that God bestows the riches of His grace on us. There is no mention of another way or another person through which God's grace can be obtained.

Paul also touches on God's grace in Romans 5:1-2:

> Therefore, since we have been justified through faith, we have peace with God through our Lord Jesus Christ, through whom we have gained access by faith into this grace in which we now stand.

Paul is saying here that we have gained access to God's grace through faith in *Jesus Christ*. This faith we have in

Christ that merits God's grace is exclusive. Nowhere is it said that receiving this grace is at all contingent upon any actions taken by the Virgin Mary or any actions we take in petitioning her.

So is faith in Christ alone sufficient to warrant God's favor? Paul seems to think so. This theme is not only evident in the books of Romans and Ephesians, but in all fourteen of Paul's epistles.

If it were truly necessary for us to approach Mary to obtain God's favor, you'd think God would have revealed that to Paul or one of the other New Testament writers. Not only did the New Testament writers never mention another mediator through which to gain access to God's grace, but Paul also left no room for it.

In I Timothy 2:5, Paul says, "for there is *one* God and *one* mediator between God and men, the man Christ Jesus." This is about as exclusive as you can get.

If Paul's words aren't good enough, let's examine the words of Jesus Himself. In John 14:6, Jesus says these renowned words: "*I am the way, the truth, and the life. No one comes to the Father except through me.*" There is no other way to the Father except Christ alone.

To be fair, the Catholic Church is not saying that Mary's role in any way diminishes the role of Jesus.

Catechism 970 explains how the church reconciles its *Mediatrix* doctrine with sacred Scripture: "Mary's function as mother of men (mankind) in no way obscures or diminishes this unique mediation of Christ, but rather shows its power. But the Blessed Virgin's salutary influence on men… flows forth from the superabundance of the merits of Christ, rests on his mediation, depends entirely on it, and draws all power from it."

The Church is very careful to point out that Mary's role is entirely dependant upon Christ. They acknowledge correctly that Mary can do nothing on her own and that Christ is the source of all her power.

The problem with the Church's explanation is that they never explain how Mary obtained this position of *Mediatrix* in the first place. Even if Mary draws entirely upon Christ to carry out her role (which should go without saying anyway), where in sacred Scripture does it even imply that Mary is in charge of dispensing God's grace?

The other problem with giving Mary this special role is that it leads many of the Catholic faithful to devote far more of their time and energy praying to Mary rather than praying to God. Even though the Catechism states that Jesus is Mary's ultimate source, many of the Catholic faithful have it the other way around.

Because Catholics believe it's necessary to go through Mary to receive God's grace, millions of prayers are said to Mary every single day. In fact, if people are praying the rosary, which is a popular Catholic devotion to Mary, they end up saying ten *Hail Marys* for every one *Our Father*.

The result of this excessive devotion to Mary has been that in many parts of the world Mary is worshipped. Even though the Catholic Church is quick to point out this devotion to Mary is just a petition for her assistance in obtaining God's favor, in practice it often ends up being pure worship.

The Church will say that petitioning Mary to pray for us is no different than asking someone you know to pray for you. If you are a Christian, you likely believe in the power of prayer. It is also likely that you would believe that the more people praying for you, the better.

The Bible says "the prayer of a righteous man is powerful and effective."(James 5:16). If Mary is most righteous of all persons, her prayers would be very powerful indeed. The prayers of other saints would also be very powerful.

This is why the Catholic Church advocates petitions to not only Mary but the other saints as well. The Church insists it is not idolatry because Catholics are not worshipping the saints, just asking them to pray for their needs. The belief is that God will be more responsive to the prayers of saints on our behalf than He would be to our own prayers.

So, from the Catholic Church's official view, Mary's role as *Mediatrix of all Graces* is mostly a role of advocacy. She is the perfect dispenser of grace because she cooperated fully in God's saving work. She is also able to help us through her prayers to God on our behalf, as any righteous person would.

Even if the billion Catholics worldwide practiced this Marian devotion the way the Catholic Church officially preaches, one would still wonder about some of the assumptions made to justify this devotion.

Aside from the highly debatable issue of whether or not Mary sinned, where in sacred Scripture does it say we are supposed to pray to those who have already died?

Again, we would think that this would have been mentioned by at least one of the writers of the Bible. From Genesis to Revelation, the only legitimate prayers that are ever said are to God. There are no prayers to any of the saints by *anyone* throughout Scripture.

Some may argue that the writers of the New Testament were the first of the saints and were mostly alive when all the books of the New Testament were written. This is true, but the Old Testament also had many righteous people. Just because they aren't referred to as saints, there are many Old Testament figures that would seem worthy of petitioning if that were possible.

For example, why didn't people in Jesus' time pray to Abraham, Joseph, Moses or Elijah? These were all holy men who could have added much effectiveness to the prayers of the Jewish people of that time. The Jews certainly honored these men for what they wrote and did, but none were ever prayed to.

Some may say the rules changed when Jesus died on the cross. Even if this were true, why wouldn't the New Testament writers have mentioned it? For example, why wouldn't Paul have petitioned and given devotion to Abraham, the father of our faith, instead of Christ alone?

The scriptural fact is that no devotions ever occurred to those who had died. The one Old Testament precedent to contacting a dead person was when King Saul had the Witch of Endor call up the spirit of Samuel (Samuel 28). The day after Saul did this, he died in battle.

There is one New Testament event in which Jesus took Peter, James, and John to the holy mountain to be transfigured (Matthew 28:3, Mark 9:2). When they were on top of the mountain, Moses and Elijah appeared and were talking with Jesus. This was a onetime event and was never repeated by anyone else but Jesus.

The consequence of this practice of devotions to Mary and the saints is that, although the Catholic Church's intention is to draw the faithful closer to God, in practice it detracts from God's glory. If we are in the practice of praying to human beings more than to God Himself, we would tend to give these human beings more credit for the answered prayers than God Himself.

This is exactly what has happened with many Catholics around the world. Many of them give credit to Mary for answering their prayers. Pope John Paul II gave Mary, not God, credit for saving his life when an assassin's bullet nearly killed him in 1981.

In fact, according to catholicplanet.com, one of the required criteria to be canonized a saint by the Catholic Church is for the prospective saint to have at least one miracle attributed to them.

The first commandment says, "I am the Lord your God…you shall have no other gods before me" (Ex. 20:2-3).

Idolatry is strictly forbidden in all its forms, and it is made clear by the fact that this is the very first commandment.

Perhaps the biggest problem with this unbiblical practice of Marian devotion is that it not only runs counter to what is taught in Scripture, but it also encourages Catholics to engage in idolatry. The Church does very little if anything to stop these abuses from occurring. In fact, it seems to encourage them by its silence on the matter.

Idolatry is perhaps the greatest of all offenses toward God. In all its forms, it distracts us from the true source of all that is good.

Even when the apostle John tried to worship one of God's angels in Revelation 22:8-9, the angel rebuked him, saying he (the angel) was a fellow servant. "Worship God" was the angel's simple message. This should also be the message of the Catholic Church to its faithful.

CHAPTER 7

Queen of Heaven and Coredemptrix

Two additional titles commonly given to Mary help us shed more light on the Catholic Church's view of Mary's role in God's plan of salvation. Though neither title appears in the official *Catechism of the Catholic Church*, both are widely used and accepted by church leaders throughout the world. They are *Queen of heaven* and *Coredemptrix*.

Queen of Heaven

The title *Queen of heaven* was first used to describe Mary in the seventh century A.D. by Pope Martin. There are several justifications used by various church leaders for this title. In this discussion, we will cover just a couple of the most popular reasons for the church to refer to Mary this way.

According to EWTN.com, Mary's queenship is inherited by virtue of Christ inheriting the throne of King David. This throne is the spiritual kingdom of God and is a heavenly kingdom. Because in Old Testament tradition the mother of the king of Israel was often made queen, Mary was the logical heir to the queenship of Christ's spiritual kingdom.

Another popular explanation is that since Mary was declared the *Mother of God* by the council of Ephesus in 432 A.D., and since Mary is a co participant in Christ's redemptive work, she is worthy to be called our mother and queen over God's domain.

So what's so bad about referring to Mary as *Queen of heaven*? Some might say it's a pretty harmless title, one she may even deserve. After all, very few dispute the idea that Mary is *Mother of God*, in the sense that Jesus Christ is definitely God in human form and Mary is definitely His human mother. It may not seem like much of a stretch to call her a queen.

The biggest problem with giving Mary this title is that it puts her on close to equal footing with Jesus Christ in the heavenly realm. Mary was most likely a sinful human being, like you and I, and is being given queenship over a godly, heavenly kingdom that is flawless and has absolutely nothing to do with sin.

Certainly, Mary has been redeemed by Christ's blood on the cross and has been glorified in her heavenly body (as all the elect will be someday), but the Bible gives us no indication whatsoever that us imperfect human beings would have such positions of royalty in God's kingdom.

We recall from Scripture that the apostles James and John asked Jesus if they could sit at his right and left hand in His glory (Mark 10:37, Matt. 19:28), but Jesus replied that this was not for Him to grant. Jesus went on to say that these places were reserved for those for whom they had been prepared.

This exchange implies that even Jesus Himself could not change the will of God the Father, even if He wanted to. If it was Mary's role to be *Queen of heaven* and reign over God's creation, this would certainly have shown up somewhere in Scripture. God would have stated clearly through His Word if He had reserved such a place for Mary.

Another problem with the *Queen of heaven* title is its pagan roots. Many different pagan cultures throughout the centuries have worshipped a goddess of fertility. This goddess has been known by many different names, but has been universally known as the *Great Mother* or *Queen of heaven.*

Even some misguided Israelites from the Old Testament worshipped this goddess during the time of the prophet Jeremiah (Jeremiah 44). During this time period, God promised to bring disaster to these stubborn people.

Their great sin was burning incense and offering sacrifices to the *Queen of heaven.* God dealt very harshly with all these forms of idolatry, as the Israelites eventually came to realize.

I'm not saying that Catholic devotion to Mary, *Queen of heaven*, replaced pagan devotion to the fertility goddess. There really isn't enough historical evidence to support that claim. I am saying that the use of this familiar title probably made it easier for pagans, after coming to Christianity, to engage in excessive Marian devotion.

Also, there is very little evidence that the Church ever did anything to stop these pagans from their Marian devotion. In fact, as the centuries have passed and the further removed we become from the first century apostles, the more Mary's role increases within the Church.

The bottom line is that there is no Scriptural evidence to indicate that the title of *Queen of heaven* belongs to any human being. It puts Mary on par with Christ Himself and gives the false impression that Mary is actually divine.

The Catholic Church would never want to give this impression, but the problem is that they do very little to educate the millions of loyal Catholics around the world to the dangers of excessive devotion to Mary.

Coredemptrix

The title of *Coredemptrix* is another unofficial title that is widely used by Catholics worldwide to describe Mary. This title originated in the fifteenth century and was used by pope Pius X in 1908 to describe Mary. Like *Queen of heaven*, the title of *Coredemptrix* is not used in the official *Catechism of the Catholic Church*.

The doctrine of Mary as *Coredemptrix* is the most controversial of all potential Catholic Marian dogmas and is the culmination of Mary's progression throughout church history from God's humble, lowly, handmaid to being a partner in Christ's redemptive work of salvation.

If this doctrine were ever to become official Catholic dogma, it has the potential to cause irreparable damage to the Church's ecumenical movement and greatly confuse the widely accepted biblical understanding that salvation is only attainable through Christ alone.

On August 25, 1997, *Newsweek* Magazine published an article describing a large movement and petition within the Catholic Church to declare Mary "Coredemptrix, Mediatrix, and Advocate for all Christians." The terms *Mediatrix* and *Advocate* already appear in the Church's official Catechism, but *Coredemptrix* does not. This petition was signed by millions of Catholics and submitted to Pope John Paul II for approval.

According to catholicsource.net, this movement has had many prominent supporters, including the late Mother Theresa, the late Cardinal John O'Connor, the late Cardinal Jaime Sin of the Philippines, as well as "over 480 bishops including 40 cardinals; prominent lay leaders and ordinary faithful from all parts of the world."

This petition was signed by millions of Catholics and submitted to Pope John Paul II for approval. Although he was a great supporter of the Marian movement, Pope John Paul

II never acted on the petition. His successor, Pope Benedict XVI is also a great supporter of Mary. As of this writing, he also has not acted on the *Coredemptrix* petition.

Here is a description of the petition submitted to the Pope taken again from catholicsource.net:

> When the Church invokes Mary under the title, 'Coredemptrix', she means that Mary uniquely participated in the redemption of the human family by Jesus Christ, Our Lord and Saviour. At the Annunciation (cf.Lk.1:38) Mary freely cooperated in giving the Second Person of the Trinity his human body which is the very instrument of redemption, as Scripture tells us: 'We have been sanctified through the offering of the body of Jesus Christ once for all.' (Heb.10:10)
>
> And at the foot of the cross of our Saviour (John19:26), Mary's intense sufferings, united with those of her Son, as Pope John Paul II tells us, were, 'also a contribution to the Redemption of us all' (Salvifici Doloris, n.25). Because of this intimate sharing in the redemption accomplished by the Lord, the Mother of the Redeemer is uniquely and rightly referred to by Pope John Paul II and the Church as the 'Coredemptrix.'
>
> It is important to note that the prefix 'co' in the title *Coredemptrix* does not mean 'equal to' but rather 'with', coming from the Latin word cum. The Marian title *Coredemptrix* never places Mary on a level of equality with her Divine Son, Jesus Christ. Rather it refers to Mary's unique human participation which is completely secondary and subordinate

to the redeeming role of Jesus, who alone is true God and true Man."

It should be noted here that the fact that Pope John Paul II referred to Mary as *Coredemptrix* is quite different from him declaring it official Catholic dogma. As I stated earlier, John Paul II was a great advocate of Mary, he just wasn't ready to make this doctrine official.

John Paul probably had many good reasons for not wanting to make this doctrine official. He knew how controversial it would be inside and outside the Catholic Church. John Paul knew that if he were to grant the petitioners' request, the chances of uniting the Catholic and Protestant churches would be greatly diminished.

We can see by the above description of this petition that these Catholic petitioners are very careful to point out they don't mean to say that Mary is a co-equal to Christ. Rather, Mary worked "with" Christ in redeeming mankind. Her role was "completely secondary and subordinate" to Jesus and dependent completely upon Him.

While it is certainly a good thing that these petitioners have stressed Mary's "secondary" role in Christ's redemptive work, how many Catholics worldwide would really know that in this instance "co" means "with" and not "equal?" How many of them are really going to believe Mary is not equal to Christ in His redemptive work?

It has already been pointed out that the Catholic Church doesn't exactly have a great history of properly educating the faithful to what Mary's proper role in the Church should be.

Millions of Catholics worldwide already practice excessive devotion to Mary by saying prayers directly to her and giving her glory that belongs to God to the point of bordering on idolatry. Even though the Church position is that they are "petitioning" Mary to pray to God for us, the practice of many Catholics is to ask Mary for miracles, healings, and other requests and attributing answered prayer directly to Mary.

Imagine what would happen if the church introduced the *Coredemptrix* doctrine as official Catholic dogma. The effect would most likely be a major increase in worldwide devotion to Mary.

The term itself would imply equality to God, and it would be up to the Vatican to make sure the faithful around the world were properly educated to its true meaning. Even if the Vatican was motivated to make sure this education happened, it would be very difficult to put into practice, especially in many third world and developing countries where Mary is already seen as almost a goddess.

Aside from the effect of such a doctrine, the more important question is does Mary really deserve such a title? In other words, did Mary play a role, even a small or "secondary" role in Christ's redemptive work at the cross? To answer this, we must refer back to Scripture.

The petitioners for this doctrine use John 19:26 as a justification of their position, saying that Mary suffered intensely along with Christ by being at the foot of the cross during His death.

Of course, Mary suffered intensely, as any good mother would if they saw their son being put to death in this manner. The question is; was her suffering as a mother watching her son die part of Christ's suffering for the sins of humanity?

Jesus Christ was flogged repeatedly, beaten, and forced to carry this heavy cross for about three miles before being nailed to it. For a better picture of how much He actually suffered, see Mel Gibson's movie *The Passion of the Christ*.

The point being that Jesus' suffering was beyond our comprehension. Also, since Jesus was without sin, He was shedding innocent blood, which was a necessary sacrifice to pay for all of the sins of humanity.

Because Jesus was without sin, He *alone* was in a unique position to be our redeemer. There was no one else that could do what Christ did for us. This is why the New Testament refers to Jesus Christ hundreds of times and testifies throughout that we receive redemption through Christ alone.

Mary did play a unique role in helping bring about this redemption on the cross. She cooperated with God by agreeing to be His vehicle to bring Jesus into the world.

Also, she faithfully raised Jesus to the best of her ability. She faithfully stood by Jesus at the foot of the cross while He suffered and died. For this, she is without a doubt deserving of being called the most blessed among women.

But did Mary in any way participate in Christ's sufferings for the sins of the world? She did suffer greatly at the foot of the cross, but so did John and the three other women that were there. Did she shed any blood? If she did, there is no mention of it in Scripture.

Even if she did shed blood at the foot of the cross, it was likely not innocent blood because she was likely not without sin. If Mary was not without sin, how could she even have played a secondary role in Christ's redemptive work? It would be impossible. For how can a sinner help redeem the sins of the world? It makes no sense.

It is true that nothing is impossible with God. But, if God would have ordained Mary as *Coredemptrix*, He would have revealed it to the early apostles so they could have written it into the New Testament.

The truth is that not one word is written in the Scriptures about anyone else but Christ being our redeemer. If Mary played even a small role in Christ's redemptive work, you would think at least one of the early apostles would have received this revelation.

Because of the clearly controversial nature of the proposed doctrine of *Coredemptrix*, the Catholic Church would be wise to decline the request of those petitioning to make this official Catholic dogma. It would be damaging to the faith of many Catholics and encourage increasingly idolatrous practices among many parts of the Church.

CHAPTER 8

The Apparitions of Mary

Over the past two millennia, there have been literally thousands of reported sightings of the Virgin Mary by Catholics in different countries throughout the world. During the past century, they have vastly increased in frequency. These appearances are referred to as apparitions.

In this chapter, we are going to examine these reported apparitions and their affect on the Church's continually evolving doctrines regarding Mary.

Every year, millions of followers of Mary visit sites where Mary is believed to have appeared to one or more of the faithful. These sites are all over the world.

One of the most popular is Guadalupe, Mexico, where it is reported that fifteen to twenty million people visit every year. The shrine they visit is called Our Lady of Guadalupe, and it is believed to be the site where the Virgin Mary appeared to Juan Diego in 1531 A.D.

Another very popular apparition site is Medjugorje, Bosnia, located in the former Yugoslavia. Millions of faithful have also visited this site since the reported apparitions began in 1981. At this site, many have reported seeing miraculous occurrences such as healings, signs and wonders, and Mary herself speaking to them.

These are just a couple examples of the many sites visited in large numbers every year by Mary's faithful. There are hundreds of them all over the world. Many of them have churches or shrines dedicated to the Virgin Mary.

These apparitions have become a worldwide phenomenon that is attracting the interest of a growing number of Catholics (and even some Protestants) every year.

The Catholic Church takes these reported apparitions very seriously. Every one that is reported undergoes a thorough investigation to determine its validity. During these investigations, the Church has determined that many of these reported apparitions are unsubstantiated. Others may have some merit, but not enough proof to accept as real.

Through this investigation process, the Church is able to eliminate the majority of these reported appearances as lacking sufficient evidence to validate their claims. What remains are the appearances that have undergone the intense scrutiny of Catholic Church investigations and are accepted by the church as having really taken place.

When considering Mary's true role in God's plan for salvation, these apparitions simply can't be ignored. There are far too many of them. Even after the Church filters out the majority of reported appearances as invalid or not able to make a decision, there are still too many Church accepted appearances to be ignored.

There are so many people reportedly seeing the Virgin Mary and hearing her speak to them that *something* must be happening. It is highly unlikely that these people would all be making this up. They must be seeing some kind of vision of Mary, and she must be saying something to them. The question is, who is this Mary and what is she saying to those she appears to?

If this is truly the Virgin Mary speaking to the faithful, then what she is telling them should match up with the Word of God. As the apostle Paul says "even if we or an angel from heaven should preach a gospel other than the one we preached to you, let him be eternally condemned!"(Gal. 1:8).

John also reaffirms this point in his first epistle:

> Dear friends, do not believe every spirit, but test the spirits to see whether they are from God, because many false prophets have gone out into the world. This is how we recognize the Spirit of God: Every spirit that acknowledges that Jesus Christ has come in the flesh is from God, but every spirit that does not acknowledge Jesus is not from God. This is the spirit of the antichrist, which you have heard is coming and even now is already in the world
> (1 John 4:1-3)

Let's take a look at some of Mary's words from various Church approved apparitions to see if they match up with the Word of God. First, here are some of Mary's words from her most popular Church approved apparition at Guadalupe in 1531. The words were spoken to St. Juan Diego as Mary was telling Juan to ask the local bishop to build a church on that site in her honor:

> Here I will hear their weeping, their complaints and heal all their sorrows, hardships and sufferings. And to bring about what my compassionate and merciful concern is trying to achieve, you must go to the residence of the Bishop of Mexico and tell him that I sent you here to show him how strongly I wish him to build me a temple here on the plain;

> Listen to me, my youngest and dearest son, know for sure that I do not lack servants and messengers

to whom I can give the task of carrying out my words, who will carry out *my* will. But it is very necessary that you plead my cause and, with your help and through your mediation, that *my* will be fulfilled. My youngest and dearest son, I urge and firmly order you to go to the bishop again tomorrow. Tell him in *my* name and make him fully understand *my* intention that he start work on the chapel *I'm* requesting.

Am I not here, I, who am your Mother? Are you not under *my* shadow and protection? Am *I* not the source of your joy? Are you not in the hollow of *my* mantle, in the crossing of *my* arms? Do you need anything more? Let nothing else worry you, disturb you.

The recurring theme in Mary's words to Juan Diego seems to be carrying out *her* will. It was supposedly Mary's will to build a temple in *her* honor. Then she goes on to say that *she* is the source of Juan's joy. He needs nothing more. As long as he has Mary, nothing else should worry or disturb him.

What seems to be lacking in Mary's words is any focus on God. All the focus is on what *she* can and will do for them if they build this church. The Bible says that God alone is the source of our joy. As Christians, we are taught to seek and do *God's* will, not Mary's will.

Let's look at Mary's words from another popular Church approved apparition. This was Mary's appearance to three children in 1917 at Fatima, Portugal. The three children's names were Lucia, Jacinta, and Francisco. Mary appeared to these children from May through October of 1917.

During the first visit, Mary said, "I have come to ask you to come here for six months on the 13th day of the month, at this same hour. Later I shall say who I am and what I desire.

And I shall return here yet a seventh time." Lucia responded by asking Mary if they would go to heaven.

Mary told her that she and Jacinta would go to heaven, but Francisco needed to say many rosaries first. Now, this is a fairly easy question to answer. Does the Bible say anything about needing to say a certain amount of rosaries before going to heaven?

In fact, does the Bible require that any certain prayer be said a certain number of times before going to heaven? The answer is obviously no.

There truly is no requirement of saying or doing any type of work at all to get to heaven. The only requirement is to believe in and receive Jesus Christ as personal Lord and Savior, and then publicly confess that through baptism.

His death on the cross was and is the perfect atonement for our sins. Beyond accepting Christ, nothing further is required. The Bible is very clear on that.

The Mary of Fatima went on to tell the children, "You have seen hell where the souls of poor sinners go. To save them, God wishes to establish in the world devotion to my Immaculate Heart. If what I say to you is done, many souls will be saved and there will be peace."

The bottom line seems to be that if the people of the world would just devote themselves to praying to Mary, the world would be at peace and sinners would be saved from hell.

The Catholic Church would argue that Mary was acting as a representative of God, as an angel would. They would say that by turning their hearts toward Mary, people would ultimately be turning their hearts toward God.

The problem is that any time an angel appeared in Scripture, their focus was always to glorify God. They *never* made requests to build temples in their honor or promises that prayers to them would end the world's problems.

In chapter seven, I mentioned the last recorded angelic appearance in Scripture from the book of Revelation

(Apocalypse). The angel of the Lord appeared to John and revealed to him many words of Jesus and visions about the future.

After John had heard and seen these things, he fell down to worship at the feet of the angel. The angel rebuked John, saying he (the angel) was a fellow servant. He then told John to "worship God " (Rev. 22:9).

To the best of my knowledge, the Mary in these apparitions has *never* rebuked the faithful for worshipping her and told them instead to worship God, even though excessive devotion to her is clearly a problem with many Catholics.

Instead, this Mary has done quite the opposite. She has encouraged more devotion to her and promised great rewards to humanity for this behavior.

This Mary has made an even bolder request in her more recent apparitions. In a message given to Ida Peerdeman in 1954, she asked for the church to declare her *Coredemptrix*.

Just as the earlier apparitions promise world peace from praying rosaries, this recent apparition promises world peace from the *Coredemptrix* declaration. It's basically the same theme: the more the focus is on Mary, the more at peace the world will be.

At the same time, the more focus the world gives to Mary, the less focus it gives to Jesus. The Catholic Church would never intend this to happen, but in practice it's already happening.

If people believe that all they need to do is say the rosary repeatedly to get to heaven and keep sinners from hell, people are going to be at the very least distracted, if not turn away completely, from the real way to salvation: faith in Jesus Christ alone. Because the messages by Mary in these supposed apparitions focus mostly on herself and very little on the saving power of Christ and God, it can be strongly argued that this is not the Mary of the Bible. The Mary in these apparitions is probably a false Mary.

This false Mary is going around performing signs, wonders, and healings in an attempt to "deceive even the elect, if that were possible" (Matt. 24:24). She mixes enough truth in with the deception to capture the hearts of many.

Just as the devil masquerades as an angel of light, this false Mary is charming the faithful into increased devotion to her, promising greater rewards if they do as she says.

Compare this false Mary to the Mary in sacred Scripture. The Mary of Scripture was God's humble, faithful servant and willingly became the vehicle through which God would bring the Savior into the world. After Mary performed her God-given tasks faithfully, she faded into the background as Jesus took center stage at the beginning of His ministry.

We can see by the number of references to her in the Gospels that Mary did not play a large role in Jesus' ministry. For example, in the gospel of John, Mary only appears twice. Once at the wedding of Cana (beginning Jesus' earthly ministry), and the other time at the foot of the cross (ending Christ's earthly ministry).

In the book of Acts, the only real history we have of the early Church, Mary is never mentioned. Peter, John, and Paul were the major players in building the early Church.

Mary is also never mentioned by name in any of the New Testament epistles. Even John, who took Mary into his home after Jesus' death, never mentioned Mary by name in any of his three recorded letters. Mary was very likely content in a quiet support role during the days of the early Church.

This humble and faithful Mary of the New Testament would never make the kind of statements this false Mary is supposedly making. If the real Mary were to appear, she would probably tell the faithful to stop giving to her the glory that belongs to God. She would likely compare her role to that of John the Baptist. After fulfilling his role of "preparing the way for the Lord," (John 1:23) John the Baptist faded into the background with these profound words "He (Jesus) must increase, I must decrease" (John 3:30).

CHAPTER 9

In Pursuit of the Truth

After analyzing what we've explored in the previous eight chapters, each person must decide what they believe to be the truth. We should all be in continual pursuit of the truth, wherever that leads.

Obviously, our particular perspectives are going to have an influence on how we view these issues. However, we need to take an objective view of Mary's role in salvation as much as possible. Failure to do so could leave us vulnerable to deception.

After this exploration into the role of Mary in salvation, we must again address the fundamental questions that are at the heart of this issue: 1) Can we place Catholic dogma and "infallible" papal proclamations on the same level as sacred Scripture? 2) If the answer to our first question is no, (as I believe we have established) does the Catholic Church's doctrines regarding Mary in any way contradict sacred Scripture?

To answer the first question, we must go back to our discussion in chapter one regarding the authority of Scripture versus the Church. If you are a person who is not open to the idea that the Catholic Church may in fact be a fallible human institution, then I'm afraid there is very little I can tell you at this point that will change your mind.

For the rest of you, I believe that there is ample evidence to demonstrate the fallibility of the Church. At the same time, I believe there exists almost no evidence to show that the Bible is at all fallible.

As I mentioned in chapter one, the Catholic Church is a great institutional and religious authority that has existed for almost two thousand years. They are deserving of great respect and reverence. The *Catechism of the Catholic Church* is full of truth about God the Father, Son, and Holy Spirit. In fact, the Catechism follows very closely with the Nicene Creed, one of the core doctrines of every legitimate branch of Christianity.

To their credit, the Catholic Church holds very closely to these truths and does not waver from them. The virgin birth, Holy Trinity, and Jesus' divinity are among the foundational truths of the Church. While some Protestant denominations have compromised these and other core beliefs to satisfy the whims of society, the Catholic Church has stood firm in spite of whatever criticism they may receive from the world.

The Vatican's strong stand on core doctrines and controversial issues of our day is certainly very commendable. The pope and cardinals are holy men of God who put a lot of thought and prayer into what they say and where they stand. Their proclamations should certainly not be taken lightly. But at the same time, these positions cannot merely be accepted without question as the gospel truth.

The reason the Catholic Church's declarations can't be accepted as "infallible" is that, despite all the great things they've done and stood for, the Church has a proven track record throughout the centuries of being capable of making errors. The Church itself has also contradicted its own infallibility doctrine.

In contrast to Church traditions and doctrines, sacred Scripture *never* changes. It is impossible for it to change. There is no way to write another book with the same authority as the Bible because there is no way for any subsequent writings to meet the strict criteria that was required for a writing to be included in the canon of Scripture.

The Bible has stood the test of time. It has been the standard of truth by which everything else has been measured for the last two to four thousand years. Heretical books like *The DaVinci Code* will come and go, but the Bible will always be there. Good writings like the Catechism will change from time to time as a new doctrine is developed, but the Bible will *never* change.

For these reasons and many others, I accept the Bible as *the* final authority on any subject. It is undoubtedly God's truth. If anyone says anything that contradicts it, that person is wrong, period. It doesn't matter if it's the pope or an angel from heaven, if what is said does not match up with sacred Scripture, it is not the truth.

The second question is not as easy to answer. I do believe the Catholic Church's doctrines of Mary and the way Marian devotion is practiced worldwide contradicts some fundamental principles of Scripture. The Church and its apologists will argue that Marian doctrine is implied in certain places of scripture and the Church has simply developed the doctrine since shortly after the time of the apostles. This is simply not the case.

The Church's belief that Mary lived her entire life as a sinless human being is a direct violation of the Bible's teaching that everyone has sinned and fallen short of God's glory. In a way, this belief also diminishes Christ's uniqueness as being the *only* human being to live a perfect, sinless life.

Prayer and devotion to Mary is another violation of biblical principles. Throughout the Bible, it is taught that God alone is worthy of praise and glory. Jesus' main commandment was to "love the Lord your God with all your heart, soul, and mind" (Matt. 22:37). Devotion has been reserved for God alone and no one else.

There are also no non-divine intermediaries listed in the Bible. In fact, Jesus is the *only* mediator between God and man (1Timothy 2:5). The Bible makes no allowance for praying to or petitioning dead saints for our needs. It is true that at times in Scripture people asked others to pray for them, but the person being asked to pray was always *alive*.

To say that Church doctrines on Mary are *implied* in Scripture is simply not strong enough to call these doctrines legitimate when they are opposed to clearly explained doctrines of Scripture. Also, for those who argue that Marian devotion has been popular since nearly the beginning of the Church, there is very little evidence to support this claim.

The truth is that even by the time of the Council of Nicea in 325 A.D., the Church's core doctrines included very little about Mary. The proof is that the Nicene Creed, the document that was developed from that council, only mentions the fact that Jesus was "born of the Virgin Mary." Think about it. Even nearly three hundred years after Jesus' death and resurrection, the early Church still had the Virgin Mary's role in proper perspective. The only mention she received in the creed was that she was God's vehicle from which He chose to bring the Savior into the world.

Given the many holes in the Catholic Church's justification for its doctrines of Mary, it's incumbent upon all of us to prayerfully consider whether or not these doctrines match up with sacred Scripture. If we open our hearts to God and ask Him to reveal His truth on these issues, we can be sure that God will answer us.

CHAPTER 10

Why the Truth Matters to Our Salvation

Some may ask, even if following the Catholic Church's teaching on devotion to Mary is false, does it really matter to our salvation? That is a very valid question. Even if praying to Mary does not match up with biblical truth, how does it really harm me?

Other faithful Catholics pray to Mary all the time and seem to be very spiritual people that live righteous lives, serving God and humanity. Many of the faithful also believe that Mary answered their prayers and kept them safe or healed a sick relative. These are difficult questions that we will try to answer in this final chapter.

So what is really so harmful about praying to Mary? In today's age of moral relativism, it's easy to just say "whatever works for you is fine." If praying to Mary, (or Allah or Buddha for that matter) makes your life better, then why try to change your mind? These would be very valid arguments if all we were trying to accomplish was be as close to nirvana as possible in this earthly life.

There is something, however, that is far more important than anything we can possibly achieve in this life. Even more important than our physical health, mental and emotional stability, or how much money we will have when we retire. It's our eternal future.

Although many don't like to think about it, each of us has one. The choices we make in this life determine what our eternal future will look like.

Jesus said, "What does it profit a man to gain the whole world, and lose his soul" (Matt. 16:26). Our accomplishments here, even those that seem noble, are ultimately meaningless if we fail to make one critical choice: to receive Jesus Christ as our Lord and Savior.

The decision to receive Christ has consequences. It requires a commitment to follow Christ's teachings and do God's will. In Matthew 7:21-23, Jesus emphasized the importance of knowing Him and following God's will:

Not everyone who says to me 'Lord, Lord,' will enter the kingdom of heaven, *but only he who does the will of my Father who is in heaven. Many* will say to me, 'Lord, Lord,' did we not prophesy in your name and in your name drive out demons and perform many miracles? Then I will tell them plainly, '*I never knew you.* Away from me you evildoers.'

This is obviously a very scary scenario that will be played out by many people who think they are saved. Can you imagine living your whole life thinking you've done everything you need to do to get into heaven, only to realize after it's too late that getting into heaven has *nothing* to do with anything you did and *everything* to do with knowing Christ and following God's will?

Unfortunately, there are many people who think that what is required to get into heaven is to say enough rosaries, be involved in enough volunteer activities, or show up in church every Sunday. This is a common belief among Christians of all denominations, not just Catholics. If asked, many would profess to believe in salvation through Christ alone, but their actions say something entirely different.

Thankfully, we no longer need to be confused about this issue. Jesus' words in Matthew 7:21-23 indicate that eternal salvation is really about knowing Christ and doing God's will.

Praying to Mary or listening to the words of the false Mary in the apparitions does nothing to help us accomplish either of these two objectives. In fact, they do just the opposite.

Many in the Catholic Church would argue that Mary "points the way" to Jesus and would therefore be helpful in getting to know Christ. That's a nice theory, but in practice, the only person Mary really points the way to is herself. The increasing worldwide devotion to Mary has done nothing to glorify God. It has done nothing to point people to salvation through Jesus Christ. Quite the opposite has happened. Mary devotion leads to more dependence upon Mary.

It is now to the point where many faithful Catholics believe Mary is the way into the kingdom of heaven, praying to her ten times as often as to God.

Those who practice this kind of Marian devotion may claim to have peace, spirituality and even prosperity in their lives, but very often their eternal future is in jeopardy without them even knowing it!

God's Plan for our Salvation

I believe that for Catholics and Protestants alike practicing more devotion to Mary than to God Himself is, at the very best, totally unnecessary, and at the very worst, outright idolatry.

It is very clear from sacred Scripture that God has given us no requirements to petition or pray to human beings that have already died. Instead, He wishes for us to approach Him directly.

God has a wonderful plan for our lives. His plan was carried out by His Son Jesus Christ going to the cross for our sins. By committing this selfless act, Jesus Christ paid yours and my sin debt in full. Nothing further is required.

What we need to understand is that *every* single one of us is a criminal. We've all broken God's laws and we all deserve the ultimate punishment of eternal separation from God. James says that if you break even one of God's laws, you are guilty of breaking them all (James 1:10).

There is no way for us to do enough to earn our salvation on our own. It's impossible, no matter how good a life we have lead. This is why even the best among us are in need of a Savior. Even Mary herself acknowledged that need (Luke 1:47).

There is only one person who never sinned and is capable of paying our penalty for us. That person is Jesus Christ. Because Christ went to the cross and took the punishment for all of our sins, we have been provided a way to avoid the justice we deserve for our sins and be united with God for eternity.

Jesus said in John 14:6: "I am the way, the truth and the life, no man comes to the father but through me." Jesus Christ is our only "way" to salvation. He is the only "way" to reconciliation with God because He paid the price for our sins. We were (and are) unable to pay this price ourselves, no matter how righteous a life we live.

If there were any other way for us to atone for breaking God's laws and receive God's justice at the same time, it is probable that God would not have sent His only Son to die such a brutal death in our place. If there were any other way for God to reconcile these issues, Christ's horrible crucifixion would not have been necessary.

Without Jesus Christ dying and paying the penalty for our sins, we as a human race would be condemned to eternal separation from God.

You see, God is a perfectly just judge. Because of this fact, He *must* make us pay for breaking His law. Just as a good judge would never let a mass murderer go free, God would not be the perfect judge He is without punishing us for our crimes.

Fortunately for us, God loves us so much that He came up with a simple plan for us to avoid our due punishment and be united eternally with Him: choose to put our faith and trust in Jesus Christ as a perfect atonement for our crimes.

It's a *choice* we all must make. There is no way we can escape it. At one time or another, before we die, each one of us will choose to either accept or reject Jesus Christ's atonement for our sins.

This choice we must make has nothing to do with praying to or petitioning Mary, because she can't save us. Only faith and trust in Jesus Christ can save us. This choice also has nothing to do with praying to or petitioning the saints, because again only faith and trust in Jesus Christ can save us.

This critical choice also has nothing to do with us praying for the souls in purgatory. We can pray for these souls until we're blue in the face, but it doesn't bring us any closer to Christ, because we are probably praying about a place that's nonexistent.

Purgatory is never mentioned in Scripture. Jesus talked a lot about heaven and hell, but never once did He mention a place where we would go to work off some of our own sin debt.

This might have something to do with the fact that Jesus paid our entire sin debt in *full* at the cross, thereby eliminating the need for us to do anything further.

This truth is demonstrated by Jesus' encounter with the thief that was crucified next to Him on the cross. If there was anyone that Jesus came in contact with that would have deserved purgatory before entering heaven, it would have been this thief.

The thief on the cross admitted he was a criminal and deserved to die for his crimes. He then asked Jesus to remember him (the thief) when He (Jesus) came into His kingdom. Did Jesus tell the thief that He first needed to spend a few hundred or a thousand years in purgatory? No. In fact, this is what Jesus said: "I tell you the truth, *today* you will be with me in paradise" (Luke 23:43). Today! Not next week or next month or after one hundred years in purgatory.

The thief was not only spared eternity in hell through God's mercy, but was also given God's grace by being allowed entrance into paradise that very day. The only action the thief was required to take was to put his faith in Jesus.

Notice what was also missing from the dialogue between the thief and Jesus—an intermediary. The thief never asked Mary, who was at the foot of the cross, to ask Jesus or God to have mercy on Him. The thief went directly to Jesus, the one mediator between God and man. This is what we are all instructed to do.

God has a wonderful plan for our lives, and it starts by putting our faith and trust in Jesus Christ as the perfect sacrifice for all our sins. If you've never done that, let me challenge you to make today the day of your salvation. Pray this simple prayer right now:

> Lord Jesus, I am a sinner. I acknowledge that I am a criminal deserving eternal punishment. I also acknowledge that you are the only way to eternal life. Thank you for going to the cross for me and taking the punishment for my sins. From this day forward, I repent of all my sins and put my faith and trust in you as my personal Lord and Savior. I give my life totally and completely to you and commit to live for you all the days of my life.

If you prayed that prayer (or something like it) with all your heart, you just became "born again." You have now been justified. You are a new creation in Christ. Now begins the lifelong process of sanctification. You will certainly continue to sin while you are in this worldly state, but God will continually transform your heart and make you more and more into the person He wants you to be. I am not promising that life will be easy, but the rewards for this decision in this life and the next will be greater than you can possibly imagine.

Although works are not necessary for salvation, if you have truly made the decision to follow Christ, your good works will be the evidence that you made this decision. If you continually seek God, this will happen naturally.

There are a few practical ways to insure that you continually seek to know Christ and do God's will. First, set aside time to pray daily.

I know everybody is busy, but hopefully you can find fifteen to thirty minutes out of your busy schedule to get alone with God in prayer. Like your physical body, you need spiritual nourishment. Without it, you will be spiritually dead.

When you pray, make sure your prayers are directly to God, Jesus Christ, or the Holy Spirit. God desires a personal relationship with each one of us. Through Jesus, we have earned the right to approach God's throne directly.

Even if you don't believe praying to Mary or the saints is wrong, there is nothing you can gain from praying to them that can't be gained one hundredfold or more by praying directly to God. God loves you. He's waiting to hear from you.

Another way to draw closer to God is getting to know the truth contained in His Word. Knowing the Scriptures will help you find out directly what God thinks about a certain subject. It is best to combine this with prayer, asking the Holy Spirit to reveal His truth in the pages of His Word.

Finally, find a Bible-believing church (Catholic or Protestant) to get involved with. As believers, we are meant to be involved with a like-minded community. No one can be an island.

In this world full of evil and deception, we all need encouragement from the body of Christ so we aren't tempted to drift away from our relationship with God.

What it all comes down to is making Jesus Christ the number one priority in our lives. *Everything* else must take a back seat to this pursuit. As Jesus promised in Matthew 6:33: "seek first the kingdom of God and his righteousness, and *all* these things will be given to you as well."

If we do as He says, we will have no need to doubt or question where we will spend our eternal future. Like the thief on the cross, we can be assured that one day we, too, will be with Jesus in paradise.

BIBLIOGRAPHY

Unless otherwise noted, all Scripture is taken from the New International Version of the Holy Bible, copyrighted 1973, 1978, 1984 by International Bible Society.

Alexander, Pat & David. *Zondervan Handbook to the Bible*. Grand Rapids, MI: Zondervan Publishing, 1999.

Apparitions of Jesus and Mary (2004, January). *Major Apparitions of Jesus and Mary*. Retrieved June 28, 2006, from http://www.apparitions.org/

Beckman, Martin. *An Explanation of the Coredemptrix of Mary Title*. Retrieved June 10, 2006, from http://www.catholicsource.net/articles/coredemptrix.html

Bruce, F.F. *The Canon of Scripture*. Downers Grove, IL: InterVarsity Press, 1988.

Catechism of the Catholic Church (Second Edition). Washington, D.C.: United States Catholic Conference, 2000.

Collins, Mary Ann (2006). *A Study of Catholic Practice and Doctrine*. Retrieved March 13, 2006, from http://www.catholicconcerns.com/MaryWorship.html

Conte Jr., Ronald L. (2005). *Papal Infallibility and the Canonization of Saints*. Retrieved April 7, 2006, from http://www.catholicplanet.com/TSM/infalli-bility- canonizations.htm

Conte Jr., Ronald L. (2005). *Papal Infallibility in Providentissimus Deus*. Retrieved April 7, 2006, from http://www.catholicplanet.com/TSM/papal-infallibility.htm.

Geisler, Norman L. (2006 July-August). Reasons For Our Hope: Why We Can Trust The Bible. *Decision Magazine, 8-9*.

The Harpazo Network (2005). *Queen of All*. Retrieved July 18, 2006, from http://www.harpazo.net/Queen.html

Macdonald, James. *God Wrote a Book*. Wheaton, IL: Crossway Books, 2004.

The Marian Library Newsletter (1998). *Proposed Dogma: " Mary: Co-Redemptrix, Mediatrix, and Advocate." Something to Consider Before You Sign*. Retrieved June 8, 2006, from http://www.udayton.edu/mary/respub/summer98

Miller, E. & Samples, K. *The Cult of the Virgin: Catholic Mariology and the Apparitions of Mary*. Grand Rapids, MI: Baker Book House Company, 1992.

Most, William G. (1996) *Mary's Queenship*. Retrieved July 18, 2006, from http://www.ewtn.com/faith/teachings/marya6.htm

New Advent (2003). *The Nicene Creed*. Retrieved July 11, 2006, from http://www.newadvent.org/cathen/11049a.htm

Scheifler, Michael (2002). *Movement to Declare Mary Co-redemptrix underway!*

Retrieved June 8, 2006, from http://www.aloha.net/~mikesch/medtrix.htm

Strobel, Lee. *The Case for Christ*. Grand Rapids, MI: Zondervan Publishing, 1998.

Tetlow, Jim. *Messages from Heaven*. Fairport, NY: Eternal Productions, 2002.

Theotokos Catholic Books. *Words Spoken by Mary at Guadalupe*. Retrieved June 29, 2006, from http://www.theotokos.org.uk/pages/approved/words/wordguad.html

Theotokos Catholic Books. *Words Spoken by Mary at Fatima*. Retrieved June 29, 2006, from http://www.theotokos.org.uk/pages/approved/words/wordfati.html

Tierney, J.C. (2006). *Marian Apparitions of the 20th Century*. Retrieved June 28, 2006, from http://www.udayton.edu/mary/resources/aprtable.html

Wikipedia The Free Encyclopedia (2006). *Annunciation*. Retrieved August 10, 2006, from http://en.wikipedia.org/wiki/Annunciation

Wikipedia The Free Encyclopedia (2006). *Immaculate Conception*. Retrieved August 10, 2006, from http://en.wikipedia.org/wiki/Immaculate_Conception

www.ingramcontent.com/pod-product-compliance
Ingram Content Group UK Ltd.
Pitfield, Milton Keynes, MK11 3LW, UK
UKHW041949230426
12048UKWH00008B/230